OUR AMERICAN STORY

Our
AMERICAN
Story

The Search for a Shared National Narrative

Edited by JOSHUA A. CLAYBOURN

Potomac Books

An imprint of the University of Nebraska Press

All rights reserved. Potomac Books is an imprint of the
University of Nebraska Press.
Manufactured in the United States of America.

♾

Library of Congress Cataloging-in-Publication Data
Names: Claybourn, Joshua A., editor.
Title: Our American story: the search for a shared national
narrative / edited by Joshua A. Claybourn.
Description: Lincoln: Potomac Books, an imprint of the
University of Nebraska Press, 2019. | Includes
bibliographical references.
Identifiers: LCCN 2018047887
ISBN 9781640121706 (cloth: alk. paper)
ISBN 9781640122055 (epub)
ISBN 9781640122062 (mobi)
ISBN 9781640122079 (pdf)
Subjects: LCSH: National characteristics, American. | Political
culture—United States. | Cultural pluralism—United States. |
Group identity—United States. | BISAC: POLITICAL SCIENCE /
Essays. | POLITICAL SCIENCE / History & Theory.
Classification: LCC E169.1 .O89 2019 | DDC 305.800973—dc23
LC record available at https://lccn.loc.gov/2018047887

Set in Questa by Mikala R. Kolander.

Contents

Part III: Stories as the Basis for Narrative

Part IV: Skeptical Approaches to an American Story

Introduction

JOSHUA A. CLAYBOURN

Over the past two decades in America, the enduring, complicated divides of ideology, geography, party, class, religion, and race have created deep fractures in the United States, each side fighting to advance its own mythology and political interests. Of course, we all belong to groups, some as trivial as fans of the same music, some as significant as adherents to the same political party. Sectarianism helped early human beings survive by identifying outsiders and potential enemies, and it remains part of our core instinct. However, allegiance to country has in modern America transcended other loyalties to unite us around shared national narratives, events, and rituals. Although healthy nations may harbor substantial sectarianism, when loyalty to another faction outweighs loyalty to the national sect and national narrative, the political system has the potential to buckle and break.

We've seen these factional clusters deepen, harden, and separate, leading in turn to anger, misunderstanding, and hostility. Meanwhile, trust in institutions—government, business, the media, and higher education—continues to erode. Cultural warfare further splits our society, exposing fundamental differences about our views of justice and human nature. Unable to agree on first principles, we cannot agree on what it means to be American. As a result, we share few of the touchstones that, in the past, contributed to our national mythology. For instance, talk of the Thanksgiving holiday or Puritans now spawns debate over genocide of Native Americans. Talk of the Founding Fathers spurs reminders of the slave system they protected. Even the national anthem causes division in sports. As we disregard or dismantle these symbols and pastimes, thereby altering our national narrative, can we replace them with stories and rites to unite our various groups and maintain meaning in our American experiment?

Should loss of our former narratives concern us? Moving forward, can we recover or create a unifying national narrative? If so, what elements should that narrative comprise? And how should our story influence the wider world? Do the changes underway suggest an existing, common, national narrative as yet unarticulated? These questions prompted me to ask some of America's leading thinkers for essays addressing our central issue—the unifying American story.

Answering the question, What is America? British writer G. K. Chesterton called the burgeoning republic "a nation with the soul of a church." Noting the founding "sacred texts," Chesterton characterized America as "the only nation in the world that is founded on a creed."[1] Later, Prime Minister Margaret Thatcher noted that America had built its foundation on an idea, but "the European nations are not and can never be like this. They are the product of history and not of philosophy."[2] Although nearly all European nations trace their beginnings to a common ethnic kinship or cultural characteristic, Americans trace their roots—most as exiles and immigrants—to their voluntary assent to shared beliefs. In 1776 an extraordinary stew of ideas and leaders resulted in the Declaration of Independence; eleven years later, an equally unique gathering created the Constitution; both documents are centered on a belief in universal human dignity. Indeed, according to our fledgling nation's leaders, no government can grant citizens the right to free speech, assembly, religion, press, protest, or redress of grievances, because such rights are inalienable. As a tool of citizens, government simply protects those rights and ensures human dignity. Enshrined in the "sacred texts," this philosophy became the American creed.

Ironically, many of those Founders who articulated this philosophy frequently fell short of living up to its guiding principles. Some owned slaves. Nearly all opposed equal rights for women. Naturally, therefore, upheaval resulted when nineteenth-century Americans increasingly contended that "all men are created equal" meant black Americans too and, a few generations later, stretched "all men" to include women.

Abraham Lincoln argued that the Declaration of Independence did not necessarily proclaim people as equal in all respects. Instead, he believed that all people possess certain equal, inalienable rights, among which are "life, liberty, and the pursuit of happiness." A free society should always strive to achieve and protect these equal rights even if, as in the Founders' case, it fell short of that goal. For Lincoln, the Declaration's concept of equality served as aspiration, "constantly looked to, constantly labored for, and even though never perfectly attained, constantly approximated, and thereby constantly spreading and deepening its influence and augmenting the happiness and value of life to all people, of all colors, everywhere."[3] Thus arose one of Lincoln's great contributions to American political science: though the Constitution is fixed (at least until amended), the Declaration of Independence is aspirational. Americans must move toward achieving the aspiration.

Themes of equality, freedom, and hope did more than merely undergird a political system; they also helped feed a national story inspiring people across the globe. While serving as a marine in combat in western Iraq, future U.S. defense secretary James Mattis stopped to chat with an Iraqi insurgent apprehended after trying to assassinate him. When Mattis gave the man a cigarette and asked about his life, the captured jihadi admitted trying to kill Mattis but said he resented the presence of foreign soldiers in his country. Mattis said he understood but would nevertheless send the man to an American-run prison in Abu Ghraib. Then the jihadi asked an astonishing question: "If I am a model prisoner, do you think someday I could emigrate to America?" An American idea inspired even this enemy.[4]

Stories allow us to discern patterns in seeming chaos and meaning in apparent randomness. A national American story arguably helped make democracy possible; it helped overthrow a monarchy that routinely seated foreign rulers who just happened to inherit the position; and a national narrative helped create the social trust necessary to institute massive social-welfare systems. An American story has the potential to unite us around a common multigenerational project and provide our shared history an overarching sense of meaning and purpose. A shared narrative and purpose can promote peace among neighbors who otherwise may not share a tribe or a religious creed.

Some modern historians call this view "consensus history" because it focuses on unifying American values and downplays conflicts. Consensus historians often view common creeds about, for instance, individual liberty or economic freedom as the unifying force; others point to tradition rooted in geography, immigration, and history. In other words, some may perceive the unifying narrative centers as assent to intellectual beliefs, but others find the binding force in our assimilation to a unique American culture. Regardless of the specific unifying source, consensus historians believe Americans agree generally about what our society ought to look like and disagree only about the means to achieve it—how much to tax, how much to regulate, and how to spread American values abroad.

Consensus historiography emerged in response to an earlier "progressive historiography" questioning whether consensus ever existed in the American story and focused instead on clashes and conflict; even if Americans shared a common narrative, they frequently interpreted it differently. Such historians view any attempt to whitewash our past divisions and view prior eras as rose-colored unity as mistaken. Events such as the Civil War, waves of immigration around the turn of the twentieth century, and the cultural revolution of the 1960s created tension about how we Americans view ourselves and our story. International wars and conflicts have done the same. Now, though, we seem to be losing any shared sense of national identity to a degree that rivals most prior eras. Varying and often mutually exclusive narratives have emerged along political and cultural fault lines so that few Americans agree on what America means and what, if anything, we can celebrate. Instead, modern public policy, political science, legal theory, and history focus on power conflicts typically between identity groups, classes, or oppressor and oppressed. We lack a central story, a common ground we can celebrate and enrich with deeper meaning.

Against this backdrop, the contributors featured here—leaders in their fields of history, law, politics, and public policy—approach the question from different angles. Even if searching for a common narrative risks neglecting some current or future group, we acknowledge that danger and still recognize the value of exploring whether a unifying story can be achieved and, if so, what that story may be.

This project, begun with an open-ended question, invites dramatically different takes. Contributions here range from skeptical to certain, from liberal to conservative, from abstract to personal. In a civic society immersed in echo chambers, one may be tempted to read only those contributions that affirm existing views. Avoid that temptation; instead, absorb and engage each approach. The diverse responses expand our possible narratives and remind us that if a unifying story can be achieved at all, then more than one may be feasible or even necessary. If you insist on common threads or conclusions, then we leave them to you to discover, and we hope you find these contributions important and illuminating. Ultimately, I aim for this project to prompt much-needed conversation and reflection.

Notes

1. G. K. Chesterton, *The Collected Works of G. K. Chesterton*, vol. 21, *What I Saw in America, The Resurrection of Rome, Sidelights*, ed. George J. Marlin et al. (San Francisco: Ignatius Press, 1990), 41.

2. Margaret Thatcher, speech at Hoover Institution Lunch, Four Seasons Hotel, Washington DC, March 8, 1991, https://www.margaretthatcher.org/document/108264.

3. Don E. Fehrenbacher, ed., *Abraham Lincoln: Speeches and Writings, 1832–1858* (New York: Library of America, 2008), 794.

4. Robert Burns, "Here's What Jim Mattis Learned When He Sat Down and Talked to a Man Who Tried to Kill Him during the Iraq War," *Business Insider*, January 10, 2018, https://www.businessinsider.com/away-from-washington-a-more-personal-mattis-reveals-himself-2018-1.

OUR AMERICAN STORY

PART I

Building Blocks of a National Narrative

1

Composite Nation?

DAVID W. BLIGHT

A man is a man the world over. This fact is affirmed and
admitted in any effort to deny it. The sentiments we exhibit,
whether love or hate, confidence or fear, respect or contempt,
will always imply a like humanity.

—FREDERICK DOUGLASS, 1869

In the late 1860s, in the wake of the ratification of the Fourteenth Amendment and anticipating the ratification of the Fifteenth Amendment, Frederick Douglass exhibited perhaps his most sanguine vision of an American future of potential human equality under law. At that particular moment of Reconstruction, such a hopeful outlook for a new American polity and society was not without credence. Douglass delivered a speech entitled "Composite Nation" as early as 1867, just as Radical Reconstruction gained traction in Washington DC politics; he delivered it on ground in the occupied former Confederate states.[1] Like some other former abolitionists, Douglass believed the United States had just experienced a new founding in the Civil War and emancipation and was in the midst of crafting a new constitution rooted in the three great amendments spawned by the war's results. He even became practically overnight a proponent of American expansion to the Caribbean and elsewhere, driven now by the new ideology of abolitionism, universal manhood suffrage, and equality before law. Douglass believed Americans could now possibly invent a new nation whose values were worth exporting to societies that were either still officially pro-slavery or riddled with premodern systems of inequality.

Might a newly forged United States, built from the ashes of a horrific civil war, slough off its former self, its earlier national identity, constitutionalism, and contested narrative as a proslavery nation, and become the dream of the authors of emancipation and Union victory? Could history itself have made such a fundamental shift toward a multiethnic, multiracial "nation" born of the massive blood sacrifice of Antietam, Gettysburg, and Andersonville? Could the tremendous resistance of the white South and former Confederates be somehow blunted and incorporated into this new vision of a "composite" nationality, separating church and state, giving allegiance to a single new constitution, federalizing the Bill of Rights, and spreading liberty more broadly than any civilization had ever attempted? We do not often think of the Reconstruction era as a time of near-utopian thinking. But knowing what was soon to transpire in American history, such a vision does seem utopian.

Douglass's immediate post–Civil War definition of a "nation" came quite close to Benedict Anderson's modern conception of a nation as an "imagined community." Douglass said that a nation "implied a willing surrender and subjection of individual aims and ends, often narrow and selfish, to the broader and better ones that arise out of society as a whole. It is both a sign and a result of civilization." And a nation, both in the nineteenth century and now, one might believe, demands a story that holds it together, that draws its constituent parts to adhere to a whole. *E pluribus unum* is a wonderful aspiration. One might wonder how the former slave who had delivered some of the most embittered attacks on American racism and hypocrisy before and during the war could now in the late 1860s believe his newly saved and reinvented country was "the most fortunate of nations" and "at the beginning of our ascent."[2] In the first quarter century of his public life, few Americans left a more thoroughgoing chastisement of the tyranny and tragedy at the heart of America's institutions, its actions, and its historical narrative than Douglass.

When Douglass returned in 1847 from his extraordinary

nineteen-month experience in the British Isles, where he had been celebrated and treated with more equality than he had ever imagined in America, he let it be known that "home" and "country" were now very ambivalent concepts. Douglass was excited to be back among his abolitionist comrades, but America was another matter. "I have no love for America, as such," he jarringly announced. "I have no patriotism. I have no country." Douglass let his righteous anger flow in metaphors of degradation, chains, and blood. "The institutions of this country do not know me, do not recognize me as a man," he declared, "except as a piece of property." The only thing attaching him to his native land was his "family" and his deeply felt ties to the "three millions of my fellow creatures groaning beneath the iron rod . . . with . . . stripes upon their backs." Only their "clanking . . . chains" and their "warm blood . . . making fat the soil of Maryland and of Alabama" drew him back to America. Such a country, Douglass said, he could not love. "I desire to see it overthrown as speedily as possible, and its Constitution shivered in a thousand fragments."[3]

Already a master of the rhetorical device of the jeremiad—calling the fallen nation back to its lost principles—but also now portraying himself as the victim of proslavery scorn, Douglass enjoyed being the aggressor. Constantly under attack for irritating Americans rather than feeding their need for a pleasing story, Douglass happily pleaded guilty. "I admit that we have irritated them," he declared. "They deserve to be irritated. . . . As it is in physics, so in morals, there are cases that demand irritation, and counter irritation. The conscience of the American public needs this irritation. And I would blister it all over, from centre to circumference, until it gives signs of a purer . . . life than it is now manifesting to the world." Douglass named the demons and stalked his prey. As the latter-day Jeremiah he spoke like the ancient prophet, calling the nation to judgment for its mendacity and its wanton violation of its own covenants, warning of its imminent ruin, and demanding a new story.[4]

Douglass had always believed in an American "mission," that the United States was fundamentally a set of ideas, despite, as he said even in the hopeful mode of 1869, its "tangled network of contradictions." His temporary optimism of this moment says much about the explosions of hope and the transformative character of emancipation for a former slave and abolitionist. Douglass admitted that he had never believed in perfectionism, but he did think the new nation of early Reconstruction now provided an aspiration for humankind, "the perfect national illustration of the unity and dignity of the human family."[5] Such misty-eyed hope! On good days, many Americans still want to believe in a narrative of American history bound up in this perception of the possibilities of multiethnic and cultural harmony. Others still demand a cohesive narrative of progress and greatness, the story of a special problem-solving nation providing beacons of light and cities on hills for the entire world to model. As a culture we have never lacked for writers, politicians, and artists who savor and recreate this triumphal conception of America history.

• • •

In the nineteenth century, no American spun the yarns of historical progress or of America's exceptionality under a Christian God's guidance more than George Bancroft. The gentleman scholar wrote many books and gave many speeches, fashioning a narrative of American greatness as the model for human unity. Educated at Harvard and in Germany, Bancroft wrote in ten volumes *The History of the United States, from the Discovery of the American Continent to the Present Time*, published from 1834 to 1874.[6] His vision of the history of America was one rooted in unquestioned faith in progress, in Providence, in the necessity of patriotism, and in democratic and republican values as he conceived them. His history virtually sang a kind of Hail Americana. To this day those who insist upon or wish for a unifying narrative of America's history and future are harking back, knowingly or not, to Bancroft and his various imitators. The question before American historians and their readers has been, for a century and more, whether "we" can imagine a unified national narrative out of our vast multiplicity, our violence, our embrace of and hostility to immigrants, our racism, our profound tragedies, and, yes, our considerable triumphs of human will and sacrifice. Such a unified story was all but obliterated in the Civil War. But the idea of America does not die; it has been too long in its evolution out of the Enlightenment world. It serves the aspirations for liberty and freedom in too many hamlets and cultures we hardly know. But whether a United States can remain unified, changing, and growing with a rich and abiding national story of renewed potency is an open question.

The muscular confidence of Bancroft's history is breathtaking, even as it seems so blind and out of place in our world. In an oration on the fiftieth anniversary of the New-York Historical Society in 1854 on "progress," Bancroft gave to historical thinking in a romantic age a set of creeds. He believed that "each successive generation is . . . wiser than its predecessor." As an article of faith rooted in ideas about nature, he asserted, "The movement of the human mind, taken collectively, is always toward something better." Whether a person's temperament is conservative, absolutist, or reformist, Bancroft insisted, without testing his assumptions against history itself, that a divine "Providence" provided "unity" in the universe, as well as "the anchor of our hope."[7] Bancroft believed that the practice of history contained philosophy and was second only to poetry as the diviner of knowledge and of Heaven's intent.

Why should we even observe Bancroft and his vision of history today in the twenty-first century after world wars, the Holocaust, the atomic bomb, the Rwandan genocide, and 9/11? If our question is if or how Americans might ever again imagine a unifying narrative of their history, we do well to look back at one who claimed to have discovered it with such certitude in the middle of the nineteenth century in a society about to tear itself asunder in civil war. Historians, or professional academics and journalists who write history in our time, by training tend to reject notions of teleology or of any sort of destiny under providential direction. Or do we? The broad public, even many serious readers of books, do not reject such notions. Most people love a story that tugs at the heart as much as the head. Some neuroscientists and psychologists have shown that we may even be hard-wired for such narratives, and our instinct may normally control our reason.[8]

People want to see themselves in the narratives they read or consume in the popular culture. Most people want to find their good ancestors. Who does not want to discover a heroic great-grandparent? On the other hand, how many of us have denied or sidestepped the personal stories of those distant kin who were not so holy? Either way, Ancestry.com may take you there. A Shangri-La or a Wakanga or an El Dorado is an eternal human dream of a past that can make a better present at least for a day or a season in imaginative fiction or a movie theater. Bancroft gave Americans who wished for it a white people's country with a glorious history and an even more special destiny. Bancroft's America was not even "almost chosen," as Abraham Lincoln once remarked, but chosen for special work indeed.[9] In the popular imagination, historical narratives are always as much beliefs as they are histories. Collective memory tends to trump history. Every person walking a street, managing a retail shop, plowing a field, sitting in a classroom, or buying stock on a computer has a sense of the past in his or her mind. We all have some narrative of who we are and where we came from. Many people do not want their favored narratives disrupted by the critical tools of professional historians. But disrupt them we must. And the good news is that many Americans still read and hunger for history that challenges them to new understandings.

The comfortable Bancroft from his perch at the New-York Historical Society in 1854, speaking after the passage of the Kansas-Nebraska Act and in the midst of the roiling crises over slavery, its expansion, and its imminent threat to tear apart the American Union, could deliver such sentimental certainties as "God gives all the oppressed" a hope of liberation, and "our country stands, therefore, more than any other as the realization of the unity of the race." By race he implied the human species, but his only mention of an "abolition of servitude" was in Prussia and Hungary. The United States, said Bancroft, was "bound to allure the world to freedom by the beauty of its example."[10] Not once did Bancroft mention the festering tragedy underlying America's very existence—racial chattel slavery as a dominant force in the American economy, and embedded in seemingly permanent ways in the nation's legal and political structures. The Ban-croftian paradigm, such a vision of a country always improving, alluring the world, heedless of self-reflection, regardless of reality and defiant truths, never dies. Each time we may think it has been put to rest it finds revival in groups wearing tricorner hats and waving "Don't Tread on Me" banners, or in xenophobia, or in corporate-style, success-based patriotism, or in an invasion of a Middle Eastern country whose history we did not know, or in the election of a black president whose own patriotism jarred loose some of the worst racial instincts of large swaths of our society.

• • •

The presence of race and slavery in the founding and development of the United States has forever been the unwelcome step-child that threatens to tear asunder the idea of an American unity. Indeed, it has torn us apart more than once. Pleasing triumphal narratives of America are almost always shipwrecked on the shoals of our tragedies, our contradictions, and our recurring dilemma with white supremacy and white nationalism. The notion of the United States as an essentially white, Christian nation of citizens pledging allegiance to a flag and a history that was fundamentally not inclusive never dies; it has been energized recently by a political phenomenon characterized by authoritarianism, racism, willful historical ignorance, worship of the god of American individualism, and a new version of an "America first" approach to our interconnected world. These ideas seem to persist and survive virtually any storm among their believers. Oligarchy, kleptocracy, and scandalous entertainment are, we may have to admit, often just easier to establish in a media-saturated age than real democracy. Whatever Trumpism may end up being in our history, and however it will be interpreted when it becomes a past rather than a present, it certainly has shown us that facts, stories, and history itself can be weaponized by politics. Of course, it has ever been thus; but we are living in a moment of acute recognition that however much the historical professions thought they had reshaped the nation's story and curriculums to the good and to the ends of inclusion, the forces of reaction are always waiting. Textbook authors and teachers are forever searching for the new synthesis, the new story, the new methods that might lead us to a "unifying" narrative made of our creeds, our conflicts, and our multicultural reality. It is possible but never simple.

For at least half a century the field of African American history has challenged and enriched the American national narrative. The most visible manifestation of this great change is now the new Smithsonian National Museum of African American History and Culture in Washington DC. The bronze-colored, four-story structure right in the middle of the National Mall, where one can gaze at the Washington Monument in one direction and back at the U.S. Capitol in the other, shows in dazzling ways and on a remarkable scale how much African American history is American history, how much the nation's story is intertwined with the black experience in all its forms. At least visually, and certainly for the thousands of visitors to this hugely popular new museum, a unifying narrative is attainable.

The National Mall, of course, tells a national story. But that most public story is no longer one only of the founders and saviors of the nation. The mall rightly emphasizes political and military leaders, as virtually all nations do. But the most national space now says the United States is and always has been a country not only of diversity but also of interconnected social, cultural, and political histories, of special achievements, and of some of the worst human catastrophes of our own making. Slavery, racial segregation, the genocide against American Indians, and the Japanese internment policy were all made by people and by American institutions. And so was the American victory over the Confederacy and against fascism in World War II, as well as the crusade to land those small spaceships on the moon with their intrepid heroes flying inside.

We are a people who wrote the United States Constitution and shaped it by compromises with slavery. We freed slaves and lynched some of their children. We passed the Fourteenth and Fifteenth Amendments, and to this day some of us still try to suppress the right to vote for some citizens because they support the opposing party. We invented technologies and machines that have forever changed life on our planet for the better, and we invented the atomic bomb with its capacity to destroy all life. We learned how to clean our air and water, and we still willfully pollute that same environment. We have been beautiful and ugly as we have ventured abroad to seek commerce and to fight for our liberty and that of people we hardly know. We are famous for our hyperindividualism, and we have been a very generous nation in times of crisis. We have almost as many kinds of patriotism as we have groups of people. We have a Bill of Rights about which we profoundly disagree. No one ever sang "Georgia on My Mind" quite like Ray Charles, unless it was James Brown. All of which is to say that "we" as Americans are an enormously complex, divided, polarized people wondering how we survive as a whole.

Among the many historians of the African American experience who directly confronted the old Bancroftian master narrative was the late Nathan I. Huggins. In his *Black Odyssey: The African American Ordeal in Slavery*, first published in 1977 and then in a revised edition in 1990, Huggins said he could not decide whether to be more astonished by the Founding Fathers' audacious "conception of a more perfect union" or by their "purblind avoidance of the inescapable paradox: a free nation inspired by the Rights of Man, having to rest on slavery." The Founders, as well as generations to follow, wrote Huggins, refused to look into their own "deforming mirror of truth."[11] Theirs was a glorious beginning that needed an endless sanitizing to hold up to realities threatening the story at nearly every turn. Republics have always been unstable forms of government; they need profound stories to hold them together.

"National history," Huggins contended, "belongs to everyone and to no one, and thus may claim a universal authority." When a nation's story becomes a "monumental edifice," protected by values and powerful interests seeking to sustain a social order it becomes a force of exclusion; it demands loyalty, chauvinism, and sustained scrutiny against its threatening counternarratives. For most of American history, Huggins wrote, the "master narrative, like the Constitution itself, could find no place at its center for racial slavery, or the racial caste system that followed emancipation." In the last half century, that "center" has not held together; in professional history and in much of publishing, the center has been reimagined. The ever-sovereign "present," argued Huggins, has made irresistible demands on the past. "The American dogma of automatic progress fails those who have been marginalized. Blacks, the poor, and others whom the myth ignores are conspicuously in the center of our present." Huggins did not doubt that a "new national history" was taking shape, and he called for its research and writing in the broadest terms. He insisted that "racial slavery" would have to be a "structural part of the foundation of the [new] edifice."[12] In the past quarter century of scholarship, textbook writing, and pedagogical reform a great deal has been accomplished to these ends. But if national identity is now an especially unsettled phenomenon, it remains to be seen whether this new American story—told through and not around the questions of slavery, race, and multiethnicity— can be the building material of this new edifice.

Huggins addressed Bancroft himself and the narrative of American progress. In his books, Bancroft did write about slavery, but its origins were always elsewhere, in Africa or among the European empires. Bancroft exonerated American colonists and especially the Founding Fathers. Slavery had been a system forced upon them; the Americans were only determined to make the Enlightenment work out its destiny. Huggins was never one to deny that a whole national story could and ought to be told. He believed we needed new Bancrofts with profoundly different assumptions and training, with abiding senses of irony and tragedy, with a willingness to see and narrate a story of freedom forged through tyranny. And the tyranny was home-grown, not merely made in Britain. To Huggins, black Americans had been part of the "uprooted" just as much as Western and Eastern European immigrants. Africans too had to make themselves into a new people called Americans. They too had made America's successes and failures. Progress was not the breath or fuel of a national history but an occasional by-product. History did not follow any natural paths; it did not have a particular end in sight. Huggins, the historian born of an African American railroad worker and a Polish Jewish immigrant, left this clarion call to our historical imaginations: "The challenge of the paradox [of race in America] is that there can be no white history or black history, nor can there be an integrated history that does not begin to comprehend that slavery and freedom, white and black, are joined at the hip."[13] To this proposition we should add the elements of gender, ethnicity, region, and Native peoples as well. Americans are joined at their many hips by history and creeds. We cannot hide from one another, in the present or the past.

• • •

The nature of unity and variety, or whether a whole human society can be successfully made from its parts or a compelling story can be forged from a pluralism of experiences and interests, greatly animated the thought of one of America's greatest philosophers, William James. In one of his essays on pragmatism, "The One and the Many," James said that after "long brooding," he had come to believe that "the one and the many" was "the most central of all philosophic problems." James contended that if you know whether a person is a "monist" or a "pluralist," you know more about the rest of his or her thought than knowing any other thing.[14] What did he mean? If only every self-possessed, individualistic, or absolutist American could read James, we would be a better people.

James distrusted absolutes or any totalizing explanation of history, human behavior, or even of the natural universe. The essence of pragmatism, in his view, was to leave the mind open to the testing of truths. In "What Pragmatism Means," he wrote prophetically: "The greatest enemy of any one of our truths may be the rest of our truths. Truths have once and for all this desperate instinct of self-preservation and the desire to extinguish whatever contradicts. My belief in the Absolute, based on the good it does me, must run the gauntlet of all my other beliefs."[15] Such a moving appeal for the open mind, for a self-willed, disciplined freedom of thought, is very difficult to achieve. It can feel almost like a Sermon on the Mount for the pragmatic mind. This James-ian premise aptly characterizes how we humans fashion, learn, and transmit the historical narratives we wish to live within. It helps us understand why we need such narratives, the good and the evil they might do. Master narratives of national histories have indeed exhibited desperate instincts of self-preservation; sometimes the result is bloodshed of the worst kind and sometimes intractable social conflict or alienation. To so many, the social, political, or racial order can seem at stake in sustaining a particular *story*.

James imagined a world in which it might be possible to tell a whole story through despite the contradictions. The natural universe compels us to consider that the "world is one," James admitted. There are laws of physics and deep patterns in nature. Gravity and heat conduction are real and permanent. "Space and time are thus vehicles of continuity by which the world's parts hang together," he concluded. But *how one* is the world, he asked, if people are the subject? To James, there were different kinds of unity. We too often celebrate the unities we find. Some things are "conductors" and some clearly "nonconductors." Those who insist that history must and ought to be driven by progress or by a particular religion or by any firm ideology will be disappointed. Those nations that have believed in their exceptional destiny, in inevitable revolution, that have reached for world domination, built ever-expanding empires rooted in commercial or racial supremacy have all failed. Some have destroyed whole civilizations in their spectacular failures. James warned about this: "Whoever claims absolute teleological unity . . . dogmatizes at his own risk."[16]

The world is actually one and not one, James argued. "The great point," he wrote, "is to notice . . . the oneness and the manyness . . . and wisdom lies in knowing which is which at the appropriate moment." James knew that much is at stake in our stories. In what he called "aesthetic union," he acknowledged that "things tell a story. Their parts hang together so as to work out a climax." Stories demand endings, and "we can only unify them completely in our minds."[17] In other words, we make stories; we give them their trajectories and their meanings, and we may fight to protect them when they are the essence of our identity. Stories that demand dogmas and absolutes will push us into false confidence. Better to assume that a sovereign, all-encompassing story ought to be imagined from its many parts as we can best know them. To James, a people and a nation of multiple origins and ever more pluralistic parts needs to find its history with its eyes and minds wide open. To the Bancroftian paradigm, the enemy has always been the rest of its truths.

If "the one and the many" was to James the greatest philosophical question, then it surely has been as well in America's struggle to hold together a unified historical narrative. Our grand motto, *e pluribus unum*, is beautiful in its aspiration. Making one from many has been our nation's quest. James did not make all this any easier. But hope lies, I think, in his premises. "Absolute unity brooks no degrees," he wrote. But "pluralism," on the other hand, "has no need of . . . dogmatic temper." Absolutists are by temperament far more jealous of their ideas and stories. In James's lovely words, pluralists allow "some tremor of independence, some free play of parts on one another." That hope for free play of parts might serve as a guide to both the advocates of a conservative vision of American progress and those who demand that our national story take a back seat to identity consciousness. We ought to think with our minds and not with our identities. As James put it, the value of pragmatism is that it "tends to *unstiffen* all our theories."[18] In the academy today, we are much in need of such an unstiffening.

• • •

In the end, any national narrative, whether it unifies us or not, is a story. Nothing drives the human imagination quite like our need for story. The famous guru of screenwriting, Robert McKee, wrote that "story is not only our most prolific art form but rivals all activities—work, play, eating, exercise—for our waking hours. We tell and take in stories as much as we sleep—and even then we dream." Such a bold claim, made in 1997, could not have accounted for how social media may now have affected or corrupted our storytelling. But McKee had a good point. He offered a caution:

"When storytelling goes bad the result is decadence."[19] If Americans now flounder in an identity-obsessed search for or denial of a unified national story, the essential issues are nothing new.

Tribal thinking is both ancient and modern. Humans are creatures of the myths by which we define ourselves—the stories we choose to live within. In 1872 in *The Birth of Tragedy*, Friedrich Nietzsche noted that "only a horizon ringed in myths can unify a culture." And in 1957 the French writer Roland Barthes, in *Mythologies*, captured why myths, like the national narratives in which they are embedded, are both so necessary and so dangerous. Myths are the encoded stories from history that acquire with time a symbolic power in any culture. Myths, Barthes observed, are those stores about which we have lost "the memory that they were ever made" up. A myth, he said, "organizes a world that is without contradictions . . . a world . . . wallowing in the evident . . . a blissful clarity; things appear to mean something by themselves."[20] In other words, myths are naturalized, assumed to stand tests of time, powerful creatures of memory and not generally of history; they can allow us to not think.

For many people, history can be nothing more than the myths we live by. Or it can be much more—mythic narratives deeply informed by all their manifestations, parts, human achievements and disasters. In degrees we can choose to warm our climate or arrest that warming. Something in our narratives and our myths is clearly at stake in such an issue. Perhaps only a species-conscious unity can ever solve the challenge of something like climate change; and it might yet profoundly alter how we think about the notion of progress.

From the 1980s American historians, at conferences and in many papers delivered to each other, have constantly called for a reckoning with narrative, with the fragmentation of the craft into so many methods and categories. So many parts were wandering about in search of a whole or perhaps no longer searching at all. We seemed perennially to issue calls for new modes of "integration" or "generalization" in the face of all the new group histories. No American historian of the late twentieth and early twenty-first centuries ever comprehended our entire craft, what he called "patterns of historical consciousness," as much or as well as the late Michael Kammen. In many books and essays, especially plying the field of cultural history and memory but conversant with everything, Kammen never shied away from and indeed enjoyed the challenge of synthesis and even finding a national story of unity. "The synthesis that we seek" (his "we" meant historians but implied all of society), he wrote in 1983, "need not be like the elusive and legendary unicorn." Kammen was cautious but firm: "Scholarly synthesis does not require smoothing over differences, and any intelligent synthesis can surely take social and ideological divergences into account."[21] Whether the public memory could truly be persuaded one way or another by scholarly syntheses, as Kammen well knew, has always been our ultimate challenge. But we must try.

Anyone seeking to pluck a new unified American story out of our current social and political crises will be greatly frustrated. But like the search for truth itself, the task is surely worth our energies and our imaginative effort. We must keep our "balance," though, to use a word James liked. Our pluralism is a living, profound fact, as James well knew at the turn of the twentieth century. Our highest aims should be "pluralism's doctrine," James concluded, "a world imperfectly unified." And Douglass seemed to grasp this idea as well about the beauty, complexity, and imperfection of human nature. "A smile or a tear has no nationality," said Douglass at the end of his "Composite Nation" speech. "Joy and sorrow speak alike in all nations, and they above all the confusion of tongues proclaim the brotherhood of man."[22] Like all dreams, a perfect union will always be unfinished and at times unreachable.

Notes

1. Frederick Douglass, "Our Composite Nationality," address delivered in Boston, Massachusetts, December 7, 1869, in *The Frederick Douglass Papers, Series One: Speeches, Debates and Interviews*, vol. 4: *1864–80*, ed. John W. Blassingame and John R. McKivigan (New Haven CT: Yale University Press, 1991), 240–59. Also delivered under the title "Composite Nation" as early as 1867.

2. Benedict Anderson, *Imagined Communities: Reflections on the Origins and Spread of Nationalism* (New York: Verso, 1991); Douglass, "Our Composite Nationality," 241.

3. Frederick Douglass, "The Right to Criticize American Institutions," in *Life and Writings*, ed. Philip S. Foner (New York: International Publishers, 1950), 1:235–36. An original typescript of this special speech is in the Walter O. Evans Collection, SCAD Museum of Art, Savannah GA, "assorted material" box.

4. Douglass, "The Right to Criticize," 1:237.

5. Douglass, "Our Composite Nationality," 244, 253.

6. George Bancroft, *The History of the United States, from the Discovery of the American Continent to the Present Time* (Boston: Charles Bowen, 1834–74).

7. George Bancroft, "The Necessity, the Reality, and the Promise of the Progress of the Human Race," oration delivered before the New-York Historical Society, November 20, 1854, pamphlet, Sterling Memorial Library, Yale University, 10, 14.

8. See Jonathan Haidt, *The Righteous Mind: Why Good People Are Divided by Politics and Religion* (New York: Pantheon Books, 2012); and Daniel Kahneman, *Thinking Fast and Slow* (New York: Farrar and Giroux, 2011).

9. Abraham Lincoln, "Address to the New Jersey State Senate," February 21, 1861, in *The Collected Works of Abraham Lincoln*, ed. Roy P. Basler (New Brunswick NJ: Rutgers University Press, 1953), 4:83.

10. Bancroft, "The Necessity," 23, 29, 35.

11. Nathan Irvin Huggins, *Black Odyssey: The African American Ordeal in Slavery* (New York: Vintage, 1990), xi.

12. Huggins, *Black Odyssey*, xii–xiii.

13. Huggins, *Black Odyssey*, xliv, xlviii.

14. William James, "The One and the Many," in *Pragmatism*, ed. Bruce Kuklick (Indianapolis: Hackett, 1981), 61. The lectures on pragmatism were delivered in Boston from November 1906 to January 1907.

15. William James, "What Pragmatism Means," in Kuklick, *Pragmatism*, 38.

16. James, "The One and the Many," 62–63, 65–66.

17. James, "The One and the Many," 67.

18. James, "The One and the Many," 73.

19. Robert McKee, *Story: Substance, Structure, and the Principles of Screenwriting* (New York: Regan Books, Harper Collins, 1997), 11, 13.

20. Friedrich Nietzsche, *The Birth of Tragedy* (1872; repr., Garden City NY: Anchor Books, 1956), 136; Roland Barthes, *Mythologies* (London: Jonathan Cape, 1967), 76.

21. Michael Kammen, "Extending the Reach of Cultural History," in *Selvages and Biases: The Fabric of History in American Culture*, by Michael Kammen (Ithaca NY: Cornell University Press, 1987), 140, 148, 153.

22. James, "The One and the Many," 73; Douglass, "Our Composite Nationality," 257.

2

National Narratives as Habits of Thought

JAMES V. WERTSCH

W hen we think of national narratives, we often think of major political speeches, such as Ronald Reagan's 1989 farewell address to the nation.[1] In it he harnessed the narrative of the "shining city upon a hill" to craft his message of optimism for an American audience. This narrative was so central to the speech that it could almost be called Reagan's coauthor, and in this regard he was following a practice widely employed by others. Figures ranging from John F. Kennedy to George W. Bush, Newt Gingrich, and Barack Obama have invoked the city on a hill story to draw their audience into a discussion about America and its place in the world. This is not the only national narrative that America has, but the fact that this diverse array of speakers all turned to it reveals just how central it is in the nation's political culture.

Analyzing political speeches can tell us something about national narratives, but it tells us little about where they get their power. Reagan knew that his audience would resonate with the city on a hill story, but where did this resonance come from? I propose that the answer is to be found in mental habits, but before I turn to this, I want to note one thing that a national narrative almost certainly is *not*. Namely, it is not verbatim memory of a story. Even the most rigid educational systems have difficulty inculcating long-lasting verbatim memory of this sort, and decades of research in psychology have shown that human memory is largely a matter of retaining the gist rather than the details of a text or experience, suggesting that something else must be involved.[2]

This alternative is that national narratives are *habits of thought*. These habits are general and flexible, if not protean, but at the same time, they are sufficiently well formed to bind a national community together. They can be used to make sense of a wide array of events, but they also are typically anchored in a particular prototypical event that enjoys privileged status for a national community. In the case of the city on a hill narrative, the prototypical event is the arrival of the Puritans in New England in the seventeenth century. The narrative name itself derives from John Winthrop's 1630 sermon to the Puritans, but it is not so much knowledge of that particular event that is crucial for understanding the city on a hill narrative. Instead, it is knowledge of a more general sort about a generic template that applies to multiple events.

This narrative template offers a schematic story line about escape from oppression and a quest for freedom, reflecting a universal aspiration for humankind that makes America a beacon for others to follow. Being socialized into the American national community involves mastering this template through countless encounters with specific stories in school, the media, political speeches, and everyday conversation.

Recent research in cognitive science on the "new unconscious" provides some useful insights for expanding these ideas.[3] This research is not concerned with Freudian ideas about repressed drives but instead is about the myriad decisions we make quickly and outside of conscious awareness in everyday life. In the words of popular author Malcolm Gladwell, these are decisions made in the "blink" of an eye.[4] Or as psychologist and Nobel laureate Daniel Kahneman writes, they involve "fast thinking," a form of mental processing that is unconscious, biased, and confident in its conclusions.[5] Many researchers now assert that the bulk of our thinking occurs at this level.

In this account, many of our decisions are made so quickly that we do not even know we have made them. Upon meeting individuals for the first time, for example, we typically form an immediate impression of them without any conscious reflection. It is almost as if our body has made a judgment before our mind ever kicks in. Evolutionary psychologists see this as reflecting the emergence of thinking over thousands of years that stemmed from the need to make rapid decisions about friends or foes. In the distant past, many life-saving decisions about whether to run or to fight a threatening animal or human being had to be made in the blink of an eye, and delay could be deadly.

Most of the time, intuitive leaps of fast thinking of this sort yield decisions that are good enough to get on with everyday life, but on some occasions, they lead to decisions that are dead wrong. Numerous studies in cognitive science, for example, have shown how poor we can be at tasks of logical deduction because we follow our first intuition rather than employing logical tools that are readily available. The processes of fast thinking that we employ readily contrast with what Kahneman calls "slow thinking," which is a mode of cognitive functioning that we often assume to be the norm. Slow thinking involves rational, effortful reflection that relies on logic and objective evidence. Furthermore, it can "supervise" fast thinking to help it avoid making incorrect conclusions. But experimental findings and other evidence suggest that slow thinking is "lazy" and is the exception rather than the rule in everyday life.

Returning to fast thinking, it tends to rely on selective information that confirms an existing view—known as "confirmation bias." Rather than making the effort to carefully consider alternative evidence and hypotheses, our attention is unconsciously drawn to information consistent with our views and is all but blind to contradictory evidence. In the case of national narratives, this means we unconsciously attend only to evidence that supports our nation's basic story and either ignore information that contradicts it or rule it out as irrelevant. Fast thinking also tends to be confident about its conclusions; indeed, it can be overconfident, and this can be problematic, given how biased the evidence often is that supports those conclusions.

If we consider national narratives, we find that the habits they rely on display all the characteristics of fast thinking. When we listen to a speech like Reagan's, we make fast judgments based on shared narrative habits just in order to follow the speech, judgments that we have no inkling we have made. We make such decisions with great confidence, and those decisions bring emotional commitment with them. In Reagan's speech, the particular narrative habits at issue were tied to the city on a hill narrative template. He also brought up the prototypical events of the Pilgrims' landing and John Winthrop's sermon, but he formulated them in terms of the grand themes of heroism and aspiration of the more general narrative, noting, for example, that the Pilgrims arrived in a "little wooden boat" in search of "a land that would be free."

Elsewhere in his speech, Reagan returned to this narrative template. In recounting an episode involving refugees who were fleeing Indochina in the 1980s, for example, he described how they left in "a leaky little boat" and were inspired by the beacon of liberty, with the first words spoken by one of the boat people to an American sailor being "Hello, freedom man." For an American audience, there was no need to use slow thinking to see the logic of the analogy Reagan drew or to consider any disconfirming evidence. Instead, the audience's shared narrative habits encouraged them to automatically understand and resonate emotionally with the parallel between Vietnamese boat people of the twentieth century and Pilgrims three centuries earlier; the two episodes were cast as the same story, different characters.

Reagan intuitively knew that he could rely on these narrative habits to guide his American audience to the view he wanted to share. Interestingly, these are habits that could not be assumed in the case of a Chinese, Russian, or perhaps even French or English audience, whose reactions to the speech would likely have been quite different. Even if they happened to know more than Americans about Winthrop and the Puritans, it is unlikely that they would be moved by Reagan's words in the way that Americans would. In fact, people in other countries sometimes react *negatively* to claims that America is a city on a hill, seeing them as unwarranted claims about exceptionalism, if not excuses for aggressive American intervention in the affairs of other countries. National narratives inevitably tie to an identity project. By relying on a national narrative to recount the past, we are not simply trying to provide an accurate description of events. We are also rehearsing and reinforcing the identity story that unifies a nation.

Narrative habits typically remain unnoticed until one national community comes into contact or conflict with another. Just as many Americans who travel abroad for the first time say they weren't aware of how American they were until they met people from other countries, we often aren't aware of the power of a national narrative until it runs up against another. I have seen this at work, for example, on numerous occasions in interactions between Russians and Americans, which all too easily can descend into contentious debate. During the Soviet years, this sometimes involved conscious ideological commitments associated with rational reflection. But in most cases, it reflects unrecognized but deeply held views associated with national narratives, and because these differences rely on the fast thinking of habits of thought, they are often hard to detect, let alone address.

A clear illustration of this can be found in discussions about the American decision to drop atomic bombs on Japan in 1945. Most Americans confidently assert that President Harry Truman decided to do this in order to shock the Japanese leadership into surrendering and that it worked. This is so obvious that they sometimes have a hard time understanding why the question even needs to be raised, and they are shocked and often offended to discover that Russians find this account to be not only false but laughable. On the basis of extensive conversations and analyses of the media and history textbooks, it has become abundantly clear to me that members of the Russian national community are united in believing that the atomic bombs had nothing to do with forcing Japan to surrender. Instead, for the Russians it had everything to do with Truman's effort to intimidate the Soviet Union and warn it away from claiming postwar territory in Europe or Asia.

This Russian account, which has stayed largely unchanged over the Soviet and post-Soviet periods, is usually met with an immediate, confident, and often visceral response by Americans. In fact, it is often dismissed out of hand. The problem with this, however, is that Russians have the same reaction on hearing the American version of Hiroshima and Nagasaki. Americans are likely to explain this away by saying either that Russians haven't had access to information or that they have been brainwashed—which again mirrors what Russians say about Americans. If pushed to defend their views, both sides are likely to introduce evidence that confirms the conclusions they already have. Without going into detail, I would note that there is archival evidence to support both versions of Truman's decision, and this evidence has been outlined by professional historians in both America and Russia.[6]

Rather than being the product of conscious reflection by rational actors based on objective evidence, these very different but very confident responses by Russians and Americans reflect the deeply ingrained fast thinking that binds each national community together. The American account reflects the city on a hill narrative template and interprets Truman's decision by assuming that things didn't happen as Russians say they did because they couldn't have: an American president would never have sacrificed over one hundred thousand Japanese just to make a point to Stalin. That would be too inconsistent with what it means to be a beacon of light for others. In contrast, the Russian national community is solidly united around narrative habits that focus on repeated threats from alien enemies and the expulsion of these enemies through heroic efforts by the Russian people to save their civilization from destruction. From this perspective, the bombings of Hiroshima and Nagasaki were obviously the opening salvo in just another episode of aggression by alien enemies, ranging from the Mongols to Napoleon to Hitler.

So what can we take away from all of this—that is, if we want to end up with something more than pessimism? First, we need to appreciate what we are up against, which means appreciating the extent to which we are all creatures of the unconscious fast thinking that guides national narrative thinking habits. There is now extensive evidence that we make most of our decisions in the blink of an eye and with great confidence, relying more on confirmation than information.

At the same time, however, we need to remember that we *are* capable of more considered, reflective thought and judgment and that they can provide an antidote to the tendencies of fast thinking. But can the insights from cognitive science alone help alleviate the dangers of fast thinking about national narratives? There is some reason for optimism in this regard, but this should be tempered with what we know about the history of inquiry into the human mind and will. In the *Phaedrus*, Plato mapped out a vision some twenty-five hundred years ago that bears many similarities with the struggle between fast and slow thinking. In this allegory, the "charioteer of the human soul" drives a pair of horses, one noble and the other "quite the opposite in breed and character," with the first horse as a stand-in for rational thought and the second for the soul's irrational passions. There is much more to Plato's allegory and to contemporary cognitive science, but the point is that we have been struggling for millennia with differences such as that between fast and slow thinking, and there is no reason to assume we have neatly resolved the issue today.

In the end, the best—perhaps the *only*—way to address the drawbacks of the national narrative habits will require at least two tools. First, it will require an appreciation of the power of fast thinking and the use of rational reflection to serve as a counterforce. This approach can be seen in the aspirations of serious historians to provide an accurate account of the past, no matter how uncomfortable their findings may be for members of one nation or another. But such efforts, however well intentioned, often founder from lack of will, suggesting that something more is needed to rein in the unfortunate aspects of our standard habits of thought, namely, a sense of humility.

Humility was a virtue of great concern to one of America's most important public intellectuals in the twentieth century, Reinhold Niebuhr. Decades before today's research in cognitive science, he seemed to be sending a warning about the dangers of self-serving habits of national thinking. This warning can be found in his sermons, articles, and volumes, but perhaps his most relevant treatment can be found in *The Irony of Amer-*

ican History, a book published at the dawn of the atomic age.[7] Addressing intractable and dangerous confrontations between Russia and America at the time, he observed, "We find it almost as difficult as the communists to believe that anyone could think ill of us, since we are as persuaded as they that our society is so essentially virtuous that only malice could prompt criticism of any of our actions."[8] This remains an apt description of confrontations between America and Russia today, well after the disappearance of Soviet Communism.

For Niebuhr, one of the keys to finding our way out of such confrontations was to have the humility to recognize the limits of our own understanding and the ironic twists that often govern national actions. National narrative habits, with all their certainty and biased unconscious predilection for creating self-centered worldviews, provide some of the biggest barriers to humility. These habits can unify us into national communities, with all their potential for pursuing noble and just causes. But they also can lead us to make biased, confident snap judgments about others, and it often takes more than just the supervisory power of rational reflection to get us out of this bind. Namely, it often requires humility. To say this does not amount to a call to give up our national narrative, something we probably couldn't do if we tried, and it is not to say that any account of the past is as legitimate as any other. Nor is it an attempt to avoid making hard but necessary decisions in the face of wrongdoing. Instead, it is a call to elevate the level of our thinking and actions by infusing them with a dose of humility.

Niebuhr's reflections on humility amount to an invitation to all of us to at least occasionally be open to the "Aha!" epiphany of the cartoon character Pogo—namely, "We have met the enemy, and he is us!" It calls on us to recognize that we are inescapably in a world of multiple, competing stories of what nations are and that these stories are important for unifying us and for pursuing worthwhile goals. But the best way to approach this world may be to infuse a bit of humility into our otherwise all-too-confident conclusions about why we—and others—act as we do.

Notes

1. Ronald Reagan, "Farewell Address to the Nation," Washington DC, January 11, 1989, American Presidency Project, http://www.presidency.ucsb.edu/ws/?pid=29650.

2. Daniel L. Schacter, Angela H. Gutchess, and Elizabeth A. Kensinger, "Specificity of Memory: Implications for Individual and Collective Remembering," in *Memory in Mind and Culture*, ed. Pascal Boyer and James V. Wertsch (Cambridge: Cambridge University Press, 2009), 83–111.

3. Ran R. Hassin, James S. Uleman, and John A. Bargh, eds., *The New Unconscious* (Oxford: Oxford University Press, 2006).

4. Malcolm Gladwell, *Blink: The Power of Thinking without Thinking* (New York: Little, Brown and Company, 2008).

5. Daniel Kahneman, *Thinking, Fast and Slow* (New York: Farrar, Straus and Giroux, 2011).

6. Ward Wilson, "The Bomb Didn't Beat Japan . . . Stalin Did," *Foreign Policy*, May 30, 2013.

7. Reinhold Niebuhr, *The Irony of American History* (Chicago: University of Chicago Press, 1952).

8. Niebuhr, *The Irony*, 24–25.

3

The Plastic Age

JASON KUZNICKI

narrative is a stylized sequence of events with an inner logic. The choice of a narrative—"This is *our* narrative"—lays claim to the logic at hand. We call it "our narrative" because we understand ourselves to be participating in that logic ourselves. The narrative promises insight into our future.

To claim a narrative also asserts that it has a significant relationship to the outside world. It's not just solipsism, and it's not some academic literary speculation. We like to think that we could test the narrative against real-world events and that if we did, we'd find it held up.

We like to tell and retell narratives about ourselves at especially important times. We return to them when we feel challenged or stressed or when our self-identity is in doubt. Narratives become ours by habit and by ritual. They are some of the key building blocks of our culture.

None of this is to say that our narratives are necessarily correct. We may always tell a false narrative. We may equally say of a false narrative that it, too, is our narrative. We may go on to infer a false logic about ourselves and our circumstances. The result is a false relationship between the self, the story, and the real world.

My claims in this essay are two: first, the most important American narrative today is one that historians call a *declension narrative*, and second, it's false. We are telling ourselves a false story about who we are. We love this story, and it's killing us.

It runs something like this, I think: In the beginning were the Founders. Capital *F*, if you please. The Founders were wise and

28

good. They gave us a system of government that secured for us our natural liberty, at least as well as that liberty could ever be secured in an otherwise fallen world. The Founders knew what they were doing, and they did it. Fans of the declension narrative will often add that God inspired them in one way or another.

The Founders limited the government. Arbitrary power? They checked it. Ambition? They balanced it against itself. Rights? They wrote a bill of 'em, where they named all the rights that there are. Anything not found in the Bill of Rights is no right at all but a socialist fiction of one kind or another. (As it happens, this is contrary to the plain meaning of the text actually found in the Bill of Rights, but the declension narrative demands greatness or even perfection in its founding moment, so there we go.)

The Founders saw that their work was good, and they rested. Taken together, the whole system ought to have lasted forever.

Unfortunately, though, we came along.

We in the latter generations did not know what we were doing, and God did not inspire us. We have lost the pure ideas of the Founders owing to our many willful errors and misunderstandings. The Civil War and Reconstruction fatally upset the balance of power between the states and the federal government. Progressives introduced a bunch of weird European ideas about governance that had no business growing in American soil.

Directly electing senators skewed things in the direction of a federal-populist tyranny. The income tax was a big, big mistake because it enriched the federal government way too well. Woman suffrage may have been a mistake as well. Then came the New Deal, the Great Society, the civil rights movement—stop me if you've heard this before—affirmative action, gun control, abortion, gay marriage, and Obamacare.

Now, I do hope that no one infers anything about my own beliefs from any of the foregoing. I am telling a story that I intend to argue against.

The essential features of any declension narrative are as follows. First, there is a founding moment. This moment is necessarily close to God. It is treated with reverence. Those within it can virtually do no wrong. But the founding moment is short;

what follows is a fall from grace. Some small but perhaps essential thing is confused, misunderstood, or deliberately botched. And from there the whole business necessarily unravels. From that point forward, history is like a complicated chain of logical deduction that inadvertently rests on a false premise. The inferences drawn grow further and further from the truth, no matter how valid the logical forms may be. Now the whole work must be redone—but alas! there is no longer anyone who can do it. And that's why we live in the mess we see today.

• • •

Like all narratives, declension narratives have consequences about how we think. Some of them are glaring. For example, in any other context, it should not need to be said that the good guys won the U.S. Civil War, even if they did fight dirty to do it. You'll note the absence of a word in the foregoing about slavery or about abolition. You'll note also the recasting of some of the singular triumphs of American liberty as exactly the opposite of what they were: woman suffrage was both good and urgent, as was the twentieth-century civil rights movement. There ought to be room to debate the New Deal, one would think, and to judge it on its own merits, either favorably or not. But its chronological order leaves little other option than to place it in the parade of horribles. Like so much else.

Little other than chronology ever counts as a guide to good or bad, particularly when it's good stuff that came too late or bad stuff that came too early. The Founders may have balked at using the word, but they did write slavery into the Constitution. Yet the terms of the narrative say that the good stuff can't come late and the bad stuff can't come early. If a narrative is a lens, then these are the lights that have been so diffracted that we can no longer see them.

Liberals, and some conservatives, will rightly reproach all those who too freely adapt the history of the United States to make it fit the declension narrative that they love so well. Perhaps it's innocent, but then again, perhaps it's not. And the compulsive search for decay gets weirder, if you care to look.

One sometimes finds the partisans of our national declension making some exceedingly odd turns in their deference to the narrative. Thus in discussions about current events I have found that declensionists will sometimes resort to the definitions of words found in Noah Webster's 1828 *American Dictionary of the English Language*, which in certain quarters has lately experienced a strange revival.

A group dedicated to this reference work has more than six thousand likes on Facebook, and an independent website—unaffiliated with the present-day Merriam-Webster—declares that "Webster's 1828 Dictionary contains the foundation of America's heritage and principal beliefs. It is contemporary with the American Constitution. It is an excellent reference for classical literature, Bible studies, history papers, and the ground work of explanation and reasoning for America's national documents."[1] Says another, "The first edition of Webster's dictionary is perhaps the only general dictionary that can also be called a Christian one."[2]

Almost none of this is true in any sense at all. The Constitution was written in 1787, some forty years previously. The 1828 dictionary wasn't even uniformly accepted in its own time; on the contrary, it sold only about twenty-five hundred copies, and its author was never financially comfortable thereafter. It's only in retrospect that we have made his work a cultural touchstone. And Samuel Johnson—before Webster the greatest lexicographer of the English language—was also a Christian moralist who composed numerous sermons.

In short, Webster's 1828 dictionary was nothing like a founding moment for the English language or of the entry of Christianity into it. It wasn't even a founding moment for specifically American English. That idiom seems to lack any particularly clear founding at all; Webster had also published an earlier dictionary, *A Compendious Dictionary of the English Language*, in 1806, though this too came well after the Constitution. A historian in doubt on a fine point of the Founders' language would do much better to consult Johnson's 1755 *Dictionary of the English Language*, which the Founders were at least potentially capable of consulting themselves. Both Washington and Jefferson owned a copy, though we can't imagine that either one of them unreservedly accepted its author's well-known anti-American prejudices.

What makes Webster worship preposterous is that—like everything else—Webster's 1828 dictionary had a history as well, and its history sits really badly with any declension narrative about American English. Webster's dictionary was a contested product of a contested time. So was the Constitution; so was Johnson's dictionary; so was—while we're at it—the Bible.

Which is also a declension narrative, if you think about it, albeit with a hopeful twist at the end. And though it's obviously influential, the Bible is not the first of the type: Hesiod's *Works and Days* precedes the composition of Genesis as we know it. Hesiod held that man declined from a Golden Age through a Silver Age, a Bronze Age, a Heroic Age, and finally to an Iron Age. The Iron Age is coming up on at least twenty-seven hundred years old now, and that feels like rather a long time. Have we reached the Plastic Age yet?

Then I remember: *of course* we've reached the Plastic Age. In yet another declension narrative, the damage that we are doing to the natural environment is not only real but permanent, progressive, and fatal. Like modern conservatism, whole swaths of left-leaning environmental activists are caught up in a declension narrative of their own, with a different origin, a different trajectory, and a different set of villains. Its Golden Age was the Pleistocene.

• • •

Our bent for the declension narrative is also at the origin of our obsession with ruin photography: Enter a once-grand mansion, a dead public space, a decayed resort, or just an abandoned sanitarium. Take pictures. Share them on social media. Watch the likes roll in.

Ruin photography has an arresting effect on us—to which I am not immune—because at some level the declension narrative is a feeling we all have in our bones. And I mean this quite literally, because ruins are what all of us one day will become. We love ruins in part because all of us one day will be just like them.

Plausibly enough, what is true of our bodies may also be true of our polities: we almost expect that we live in the dregs of history and that history itself will unwind in the next few decades at the latest. That feeling is greatly confirmed when we spend an idle hour gazing, say, at the dilapidated resorts of the Catskills, which lie just a short drive north of New York City: The ruined swimming pools and concert halls. The graffiti. The trashed offices. The exuberantly peeling paint, the flourishing mold, and the filthy standing water. We used to be a great nation, didn't we? Good God, what happened to us?

Here we see the political ecumenism of ruin porn. Conservatives and liberals alike may look on it with smug dismay: Have we forsaken the ideals that formerly made America great? Or have we finally hit late capitalism, and after us, the deluge? It would look almost the same, wouldn't it?

As with so many political conflicts, neither side is even close to correct. Three actually quite cheerful facts explain why those resorts in the Catskills died out: air conditioning, cheap air travel, and the decline of anti-Semitism. Air conditioning made it really hard to compete with just never leaving New York City, which is, let's face it, pretty nice. Cheap air travel put Hawaii in reach, and Hawaii also beats the hell out of the Catskills. And the decline of anti-Semitism, both in the United States and in Europe, meant that Jewish vacationers, always prominent in the Catskills, could go almost anywhere else they wanted. So they did.[3]

None of this fits particularly well with a declension narrative. Near-universal air conditioning, cheap air travel, and a more welcoming attitude toward all of humanity are things that we should positively celebrate. Each may bring some problems here and there—occasionally big ones—but it would be difficult to argue that any of them was a net negative.

Ruin porn may seem to confirm our declension narrative, but, ironically, it only exists because we're *not* in decline: we'd have to be way worse off for all those Catskills resorts to remain in high demand and thus in good working order. It would probably mean no air conditioning, no cheap air travel, and nowhere better to go on vacation for the typical middle-class family, especially if they were Jewish. The Catskills have declined not because we have declined but because we have become wealthier and more decent. We take more vacations now than ever before; we just aren't so limited about who may take them or where. We are even known to make side trips to the ruined Catskills resorts, break out fantastically amazing digital cameras, and upload pictures of the ruins we find. Not even the CIA had cameras like that when the Catskills were in their prime, and here we are being all goofy and ironic with them.

History both domestic and foreign is likewise littered with the ghosts of declensions that either did not occur or no longer appear even slightly compelling. One good way to cure someone of a declension narrative, or at least to make them self-conscious about the matter, is simply to review the history of previous narratives.

We've already mentioned Hesiod and Genesis, but they are hardly alone. Cicero was sure that Rome had declined; his lament—O tempora! O mores!—is a declension narrative in two nouns and two vocative interjections. Almost without exception, the prophets of Hebrew scripture hark back to a better, more faithful time, and Christians learned to emulate their practice. The true Church was that which prevailed in the Acts of the Apostles; when Constantine converted, Christianity lost something of its original purity and got mixed up with worldly affairs. Henceforth, some people would always come to Christ not for his message but for an earthly political advantage, and you could depend on them never really being good Christians. With the Church so polluted, in whom could the faithful trust?

The seventeenth-century Anglosphere pined for the long-gone days of Good Queen Bess. Rousseau pined for the state of nature. His modern follower, Claude Lévi-Strauss, did likewise—although he'd seen enough of the state of nature that one wonders why he didn't know any better. Declension is the difference between the Greatest Generation, who killed the Nazis, and the Millennials, who apparently are killing everything *except* the Nazis. (As I'm sure you've heard, they're bringing the Nazis back. Because of course they would.)

The New England colonies even had their own declension narrative, one that fell entirely before the American Revolution. In the Golden Age the Founders—by which they meant the Puritans—established a godly government. But by the *eighteenth* century, the godly government was in tatters. No good could come of a commercialized and relatively secular New England.

Yet this was the same New England that gave us many of the capital *F* Founders whom we now revere. They—the ones taking God's dictation in *our* declension narrative—*they also* liked to beat themselves up for having lived at the wrong end of a different declension narrative. They would be astounded, and embarrassed, at the reverence we give them.

• • •

A declension narrative implicates the present and the future as well; it asserts that things are bad and that they will continue to get worse. This process may be fast or slow, depending on what we do, but ultimately the narrative limits our choices, and not always subtly. The narrative gives us only two roles to play: we can guard whatever we have inherited against all change whatsoever, or we can become the agents of decay. And that's it.

Complicating the narrative—say, by pointing out that we really do enjoy vastly higher standards of living and significant freedoms that were unrecognized in the Founding era—will be greeted with hostility and suspicion. Those who hint in this direction are thought naive at best, and perhaps they are actively subversive. There are few human types more disappointed and strangely helpless than an optimist at a pessimists' party. The narrative ordains only two roles for us, so the optimists are inevitably cast as the agents of decay. The optimists may be right, and I think they are, but it doesn't help.

But to tell a narrative about ourselves can become a self-fulfilling prophecy. One who expects an inevitable doom seldom works to avoid it but seeks rather to live as comfortably as possible until the curtain falls. Predictions of doom abound. So too does cynicism: Are you still comfortable? That's decadence at work, my poor deluded friend. Wise up before it's too late!

The declension narrative of American history is sometimes offered as a call to unity, but it's so exclusionary, and its appointed roles in the present are so narrowly constrained, that declension cannot help but fracture us even further. Decline implicates all efforts at inclusion. It leaves essentially all nonconservatives, and nearly all nonwhites and nonheterosexuals, out in the cold.

As Frederick Douglass famously asked, What to the slave is the Fourth of July? A narrative that puts the Golden Age generations ago, that includes none of the people who are like you, and that declares that all changes must be for the worse can only offer nihilism to anyone not already included. It is much to Douglass's credit that he was not a nihilist, and we might have forgiven him if he had been one.

American conservatism's love of declension is a big reason why minorities in any age often struggle to identify with the American experiment and why Douglass's welcome conclusion that the U.S. Constitution was a "glorious liberty document" can be so hard for so many others to reach. If liberty really was designed by and for white men, and if they kept it only as long as they were keeping black people in fetters, then one might say so much the worse for this thing called liberty. Let's leave it behind and find some better goals to work on, like equality, or social justice.

Idolizing a past that can never be exported is one reason among many why conservatism struggles to win over minorities and why radicalism of various anti-American flavors keeps manifesting a perverse appeal. A less declensionist conservatism need not close the gates. It might insist, with Michael Oakeshott, that "the best institutions . . . are those whose constitution is both firm and self-critical, enjoying their character as the repository of a beneficial fragment of power but refusing the inevitable invitation to absolutism."[4] The absolutism Oakeshott feared can be understood both as unchecked political power and as the ideological absolutism that claims to have discerned a fully perfected system of governance anywhere in this perpetually messy and complicated world.

Abandoning the declension narrative need not and should not mean embracing its equally wrong opposite, which is sometimes termed Whig History: the view that things have always and inevitably tended to get better and that we—proud products of this process—are free to do as we like, confident that it will always work out for the best.

This view is likewise unhistorical and unprincipled. To let go of the idea of automatic progress, and to let go of the declension narrative that has been my primary target here, is to kill the false god of chronology so that principles of any sort may live. A conservatism without declension and a liberalism without Whiggishness can each find room for common ground, or at least for civil debate, which will not happen when the one looks perpetually to the past and the other looks perpetually to the next and latest thing.

Notes

1. http://webstersdictionary1828.com/.

2. https://www.swordsearcher.com/bible-study-library/webster-1828-dictionary.html.

3. Brandon Presser, "The Ghost Hotels of the Catskills," *Daily Beast*, August 25, 2014, https://www.thedailybeast.com/the-ghost-hotels-of-the-catskills.

4. Michael Oakeshott, "The Political Economy of Freedom," in *Rationalism in Politics and Other Essays* (Indianapolis: Liberty Fund, 1991), 389.

4

In Pursuit of an Idea

America's Ongoing Quest

ALI WYNE

Even where people hate American policies, there is a notion
of America that transcends that hatred: the idea of a country
where people can be who they are and say what they think;
where they are basically treated fairly, whatever their race
or religion; where the justice system is not corrupt; where
the powerful obey the law and are punished when they don't;
where refugees and immigrants can become as much a part of
society as the descendants of its first settlers. When America
is blamed for compromising this ideal, it is because the
world counts on the country to live up to it.

—TOM MALINOWSKI, "What America Stood For," *Atlantic*,
March 25, 2017

The French political theorist Raymond Aron concluded
over six decades ago that "the strength of a great power is
diminished if it ceases to serve an idea."[1] There is arguably
no country for which his judgment holds truer than the United
States, which, observes opinion columnist Roger Cohen, "was
born as an idea." Indeed, he continues, "It is in many ways the
last ideological country on earth."[2] America is an enduring test
of the hypothesis that individual freedom can be harnessed in
the service of collective aspirations. Its experiment has been a
singular one: Stewart Patrick, director of the International Institutions and Global Governance program, part of the Council on
Foreign Relations, observes that the American Revolution was

the first such event "to place sovereignty in the hands of the people, as opposed to the person of the king—or even a sitting parliament. Throughout history, the people had been the object of government. They would now be its motive force, who by their consent and will brought it into being."[3] Thus empowered, they would undertake to secure for posterity what America's architects believed to be "certain unalienable rights," among them "life, liberty, and the pursuit of happiness." One need not have been born in America to shape its story and join its fabric; one need only accept its foundational commitment—to those "unalienable rights"—and agree to play a role in its experiment. Shortly before he passed away, the French journalist Raoul de Roussy de Sales opined that becoming an American "is a process which resembles a conversion. It is not so much a new country that one adopts as a new creed. And in all Americans can be discerned some of the traits of those who have, at one time or another, abandoned an ancient faith for a new one."[4]

The Effort to Fulfill America's Creed

One cannot help but be moved by such declarations. Nor can one ignore that America's reality has often fallen short of its rhetoric. Women were not allowed to vote until 1920. Slavery was only abolished in 1865, and it was not until a century later, with the Voting Rights Act, that the federal government began taking systematic steps to reverse African American voters' long-standing disenfranchisement. The American Psychological Association's first *Diagnostic and Statistical Manual of Mental Disorders*, published in 1952, classified homosexuality as a "sociopathic personality disturbance"; only in 1973 did the organization stop designating it as a mental illness. And as the Moroccan American writer Laila Lalami recently reminded readers, "At different times, the United States barred or curtailed the arrival of Chinese, Italian, Irish, Jewish and, most recently, Muslim immigrants."[5]

Faced with such realities, Americans have historically been their own greatest critics. To their credit, while introspection is unhelpful if it morphs into self-flagellation, it is commendable if it leads to self-correction. The nation's most famous foreign observer, Alexis de Tocqueville, concluded that "the greatness of America lies not in being more enlightened than any other nation, but rather in her ability to repair her faults."[6] Consider the progress made by the four groups mentioned above, women, African Americans, homosexuals, and immigrants:

- A recent inventory noted that "for the class of 2015–2016, women earned more than half of bachelor's degrees (57.2 percent), master's degrees (59.2 percent), and doctorate degrees (52.7 percent)." In 2017, moreover, they accounted for "46.9 percent of the total labor force" and "held 51.6 percent of all management, professional, and related occupations."[7]

- Between 1968 and 2017 the share of 25-to-29-year-old African Americans with a high school diploma increased from 54.4 percent to 92.3 percent, and the proportion of African Americans who live in poverty declined from 34.7 percent to 21.4 percent. African Americans' life expectancy at birth increased from 64 years to 75.5 years during that window, while the rate of African American infant mortality fell from 34.9 per 1,000 live births to 11.4.[8]

- In *Lawrence v. Texas* (2003), the Supreme Court ruled that antisodomy laws—then on the books in fourteen states—were unconstitutional. In *United States v. Windsor* (2012), the country's highest judicial body ruled that it was illegal to deny federal benefits to married same-sex couples. Most recently, in *Obergefell v. Hodges* (2015), the Court ruled that same-sex marriage was constitutional.

- Close to forty-four million immigrants resided in America as of 2016; they and their U.S.-born children account for roughly 27 percent of the nation's population.[9] An article published in early 2017 noted that "immigration to the United States from 1990 to 2010 . . . produced net benefits worth $50 billion a year to the native population" and that "26 million foreigners in the American labor market added some $2 trillion to the American economy [in 2016]."[10] Urban theorist Richard Florida notes that immigrants "account for nearly two-thirds of all Nobel Prizes given to U.S.-based research"; in addition, he observes, "68 metropolitan areas and five non-metropolitan areas in 33 states are home to Fortune 500 corporations founded by immigrants or their offspring."[11]

Inspiring as such progress is, though, ideals can never be attained, only approached; President Obama once remarked that America's "work is never done. The American experiment in self-government gives work and purpose to each generation."[12] When one turns again to the four aforementioned groups, one appreciates just how much work remains to be done:

- As of 2017, not even 20 percent of members of Congress are women.[13] Just under 25 percent of members of state legislatures are women, and only four of the nation's governors are women. Just over 20 percent of the board members of Fortune 500 companies are women, and only 5.4 percent of the CEOs of these companies are women.[14] America's maternal mortality rate increased from 16.9 per 100,000 live births in 1990 to 26.4 in 2015, a roughly 56 percent increase; the latter figure is the highest in the industrialized world.[15] Meanwhile, the #MeToo movement, which continues to sweep the nation, demonstrates not only how widespread sexual assault and harassment of women are but also how much damage women suffer personally and professionally by exposing their perpetrators and demanding accountability. A recent investigative report, for example, spotlighted "34 current and former U.S. Forest Service women" across thirteen states who "complained of a pattern of gender discrimination, bullying, sexual harassment, and assault by crew members and supervisors." Many of them allege that they faced retaliation for reporting such incidents, including "verbal threats, bullying notes, duties stripped, negative performance reviews, and demotions."[16]

- While African Americans' homeownership rate remained virtually unchanged between 1968 and 2017, their incarceration rate nearly tripled.[17] According to a landmark study led by Stanford economist Raj Chetty, "black children born to parents in the bottom household income quintile have a 2.5 percent chance of rising to the top quintile of household income, compared with 10.6 percent for whites"; the study also found that "black boys have lower rates of upward mobility than white boys in 99 percent of Census tracts in the country."[18] Perhaps even more astonishingly, "black infants in America are now more than twice as likely to die as white infants—11.3 per 1,000 black babies, compared with 4.9 per 1,000 white babies, according to the most recent government data—a racial disparity that is actually wider than in 1850, 15 years before the end of slavery."[19]

- While homosexuals have won important legal victories in recent years, the broad community of lesbian, gay, bisexual, transgender, and queer or questioning (LGBTQ) Americans still confronts systemic discrimination: "A mere 20 states have laws protecting LGBTQ people from workplace discrimination. Two more states protect them based on sexual orientation but not gender identity. Eleven have protections only for state workers; 17 offer no protections at all."[20]

- The administration of Donald Trump has made clear its desire to reduce both legal and illegal immigration. In a detailed assessment of the immigration framework that it released in January 2018, a pair of analysts from the CATO Institute concluded that "in the most likely scenario, the new plan would cut the number of legal immigrants by up to 44 percent or half a million immigrants annually—the largest policy-driven legal immigration cut since the 1920s."[21] The administration has also called into question the future of long-standing programs, including those that "allow 50,000 people from countries underrepresented in current immigration streams to come to the U.S., pathways for those who arrived in the U.S. as children without legal documents to remain in the U.S. to work and attend school, and the family-based system of immigration."[22] Meanwhile, the State Department proposed that the roughly 14.7 million individuals who apply for American visas annually be required to submit the social media usernames they have had for the past five years; records of inter-national travel; and past passport numbers, phone numbers, and e-mail addresses, suggesting a more intensive review process.[23]

Challenges to the American Dream

If America's history is indicative, there is good reason to believe that women, African Americans, homosexuals, and immigrants will all continue to make strides. Even so, the state of the union is not entirely well: several economic and cultural strains are challenging the American experiment—strains that had been percolating well before the 2016 presidential election.

Summarizing work by Chetty and his colleagues, opinion columnist David Leonhardt offered this arresting juxtaposition: "About 92 percent of 1940 babies had higher pretax inflation-adjusted household earnings at age 30 than their parents had at the same age. . . . For babies born in 1980 . . . the index of the American dream has fallen to 50 percent."[24] Upward mobility has long been a pillar of the nation's narrative. So, too, has the notion of "one America"; increasingly, however, there are two. Between 1980 and 2016, the top 1 percent's share of income grew from 11 percent to 20 percent; the bottom 50 percent's share, meanwhile, declined from 20 percent to 13 percent. Between 1980 and 2014, the top 1 percent's share of wealth grew from 22 percent to 39 percent; net public wealth, however, became negative in the aftermath of the global financial crisis.[25]

The acceleration of automation is likely to compound both types of inequality. Meanwhile, access to higher education is increasingly becoming a fault line in American society: George Mason University economics professor Bryan Caplan notes that "those with a bachelor's degree earn, on average, 73 percent more than those who have only a high-school diploma, up from about 50 percent in the late 1970s."[26] Compounding that differential is the growing inability of middle- and lower-class Americans to obtain those coveted degrees: *Financial Times* global business columnist Rana Foroohar reported in late 2016 that "while the average net price of college education as a percentage of family income has risen moderately for the top 75 percent of the socio-economic spectrum, it has skyrocketed for the bottom quartile, who paid 44.6 percent of their income for a degree in 1990, versus 84 percent today."[27]

Some individuals continue to believe in an ideal even if they see little progress toward it during their own lives. But we cannot expect that kind of patience from everyone: even the noblest abstractions must eventually find concrete expressions for a polity to endure. To insist upon the reality of the American Dream even if and as its pursuit is restricted to ever fewer individuals can only cause disillusionment among the critical mass of society: a dream deferred indefinitely runs the risk of becoming an illusion laid bare.

Taking stock of these economic strains is essential to understanding America's resurgent populist constituency. To focus only on the material, however, is to miss the backlash against demographic change: believing its purchase to be in terminal decline, the nation's erstwhile dominant racial group is, understandably, fearful and resentful. A recent analysis explains that

> because white male Christians are seen as most prototypically "American," they have the most to lose psychologically if they perceive America and/or whites to be no longer dominant. Given that the 2016 election featured discussions of perceived threats from religious minorities, racial minorities, and foreigners, this generalized sense of threat is likely to have spilled over into multiple arenas. For white Americans, the political consequences of racial and global status threat seem to point in similar directions with respect to issue positions: opposition to immigration, rejection of international trade relationships, and perceptions of China as a threat to American wellbeing.[28]

A key litmus test of the American idea will be the manner in which Americans relate to one another beyond 2045, when the nation is projected to become "minority white."[29] How they adapt to the continued inflow of immigrants will be another. Ronald Reagan argued three decades ago that America is the world's preeminent power not because it has the most powerful armed forces or the largest economy but because it attracts people "from every country and every corner of the world. And by doing so we continuously renew and enrich our nation. . . . Thanks to each wave of new arrivals to this land of opportunity, we're a nation forever young, forever bursting with energy and new ideas, and always on the cutting edge, always leading the world to the next frontier."[30] The American idea would suffer irreparable damage were America to relinquish its openness; it is concerning, then, to take just one indicator, that "the number of newly arriving international students declined an average 7 percent in fall 2017."[31]

The Future

As has been true during every previous period of domestic upheaval, the American idea—indeed, America as an idea—is being asked to reinvent itself. While every generation regards its challenges as unprecedented in number and singular in gravity, Americans should take stock of the mountains their predecessors have faced—and moved. The early years of the republic produced bitter political divides that often found expression in rhetoric that would make us blush even today. The British set the White House on fire in 1812. America succumbed to internecine carnage less than four decades later. At the height of the Great Depression, roughly a fifth of Americans were unemployed, and nearly half of the nation's banks had failed. The 1960s witnessed the assassinations of John F. Kennedy (November 22, 1963), Malcolm X (February 21, 1965), and, just two months apart, those of Martin Luther King Jr. (April 4, 1968) and Robert F. Kennedy (June 5, 1968). The 1970s produced the Watergate scandal and a precipitous erosion of public trust in government.

America has not only renewed itself in the aftermath of discrete shocks, including those mentioned above, but also adjusted to systemic upheavals. Consider this observation from Walter Russell Mead, one of the foremost observers of U.S. foreign policy: "As Americans struggle to make sense of a series of uncomfortable economic changes and disturbing political developments, a worrying picture emerges: of ineffective politicians, frequent scandals, racial backsliding, polarized and irresponsible news media, populists spouting quack economic remedies, growing suspicion of elites and experts, frightening outbreaks of violence, major job losses, high-profile terrorist attacks, anti-immigrant agitation, declining social mobility, giant corporations dominating the economy, rising inequality, and the appearance of a new class of super-empowered billionaires in finance and technology-heavy industries." Mead immediately notes that while he is referring here to "a description of American life in the 25 years after the Civil War," he could just as easily have been characterizing the present.[32]

Perhaps the biggest difference between the two periods, however, is today's internet-driven media environment, which heightens the salience of the aforementioned economic and cultural strains by enabling "highly tribal identities" to amplify themselves and cultivate followers "unbounded by the natural limits of the primitive landscape or 20th-century political realities of scarcity of access."[33] Whether one believes that well-heeled special interests have taken democracy hostage, that minorities and immigrants are undermining America's identity, or that those who have a different conception of the American idea are motivated by bad faith, one no longer must stew alone in anger; in the era of Facebook and Twitter, one can instantly find kindred spirits. The resulting tribalism compels a growing number of Americans to regard one another not so much as fellow travelers but as hostile interlopers.

Americans are tasked not only with addressing real challenges to their nation's experiment but also with recovering a sense of optimism that they can address those challenges in partnership with one another. It helps that they are a congenitally hopeful people: as Frances FitzGerald observed in her Pulitzer Prize–winning history of Vietnam—the first such account, incidentally, to be written by an American—they "believe in the future as if it were a religion; they believe that there is nothing they cannot accomplish, that solutions wait somewhere for all problems."[34] While this unbridled optimism has proven problematic abroad—the United States has too often exaggerated its influence and believed that it can refashion a recalcitrant world in its image by sheer dint of persistence—it has been indispensable at home: it is the force whereby the inconceivable becomes attainable, which in turn becomes unremarkable. Dr. King's assassination led to race riots across the country. Just over four decades later, Barack Obama was elected America's first African American president. Close to six years before the ratification of the Nineteenth Amendment, America's newspaper of record denounced a proposed amendment to New York's constitution that would grant suffrage to the women of the state, arguing that women "have never possessed or developed the political faculty. . . . The defect is innate and one for which a cure is both impossible and not to be desired."[35] Fast forward to the present: 63 percent of Americans believe they will "definitely" or "probably" see a woman as president in their lifetime.[36]

America's progress toward cultivating the society envisioned in its creed has been halting and uneven, but it cannot be denied, nor can its people's persistence. The poet E. E. Cummings observed that "America makes prodigious mistakes, America has colossal faults, but one thing cannot be denied: America is always on the move. She may be going to Hell, of course, but at least she isn't standing still."[37] When the Bill of Rights was ratified on December 15, 1791, it gave the Constitution its first ten amendments. Seventeen amendments have been added since then; the last of these, the Twenty-Seventh, prohibiting members of Congress from giving themselves immediate pay raises, came into force less than three decades ago, on May 20, 1992. As of January 3, 2017, some 11,700 amendments have been proposed to America's foundational document.[38]

Whatever else one might say about Americans, they are invariably trying to create a more perfect union. Today, frustrated with the toxicity of congressional politics, neighborhoods, towns, and cities are increasingly acting to preserve the American idea; indeed, if America succeeds in renewing itself once more, historians a generation hence will be less likely to pay tribute to high-profile national politicians than to unsung local heroes. Reflecting on his and his wife's five years of travel across the nation, the journalist James Fallows concludes that America "is still capable of functioning far more effectively than national-level paralysis would indicate or than most people unaware of the national patterns we are reporting would assume about the parts of America they're not in." He notes that "millions of people in thousands of organizations are working toward common goals, generally without being aware of how many other people and organizations are striving toward the same end."[39]

The reality-cum-assurance that America has reinvented itself time and time again should not lull Americans into hubris. After all, what if this time is different? It may not be; one hopes it is not. As of yet, though, there is no Twenty-Eighth Amendment that guarantees the continuation of the American experiment: renewal is contingent upon action, not guaranteed by words. *Financial Times* columnist Edward Luce observes that "history is not some self-driving car taking humanity to a preset destination."[40] Indeed. It behooves Americans to take the wheel—recognizing that their nation's experiment is at risk, believing that it should be sustained, and ensuring that they bequeath to coming generations a nation whose reality has drawn yet closer to its creed.

Notes

1. Cited in Zbigniew Brzezinski, *Second Chance: Three Presidents and the Crisis of American Superpower* (New York: Basic Books, 2007), 180.

2. Roger Cohen, "America Unmasked," *New York Times*, April 26, 2009, https://www.nytimes.com/2009/04/26/books/review/Cohen-t.html.

3. Stewart Patrick, *The Sovereignty Wars: Reconciling America with the World* (Washington DC: Brookings Institution, 2018), 45.

4. Raoul de Roussy de Sales, "What Makes an American," *Atlantic*, March 1939, https://www.theatlantic.com/past/docs/issues/39mar/desales.htm.

5. Laila Lalami, "What Does It Take to 'Assimilate' in America?," *New York Times Magazine*, August 6, 2017, https://www.nytimes.com/2017/08/01/magazine/what-does-it-take-to-assimilate-in-america.html.

6. Cited in "Two Cheers for America," *Economist*, July 2, 2009, https://www.economist.com/united-states/2009/07/02/two-cheers-for-america.

7. "Women in the Workforce: United States," *Catalyst*, March 28, 2018, http://www.catalyst.org/knowledge/women-workforce-united-states.

8. Janelle Jones, John Schmitt, and Valerie Wilson, "50 Years after the Kerner Commission," Economic Policy Institute, February 26, 2018, https://www.epi.org/publication/50-years-after-the-kerner-commission/.

9. Jie Zong, Jeanne Batalova, and Jeffrey Hallock, "Frequently Requested Statistics on Immigrants and Immigration in the United States," Migration Policy Institute, February 8, 2018, https://www.migrationpolicy.org/article/frequently-requested-statistics-immigrants-and-immigration-united-states.

10. Eduardo Porter, "How to Make America Greater: More Immigration," *New York Times*, February 8, 2017, https://www.nytimes.com/2017/02/07/business/economy/restricting-immigration-would-make-america-smaller-not-greater.html.

11. "Without Immigrants, the Fortune 500 Would Be the Fortune 284," CityLab, December 5, 2017, https://www.citylab.com/equity/2017/12/without-immigrants-the-fortune-500-would-be-the-fortune-284/547421/.

12. "Remarks by the President at the 50th Anniversary of the Selma to Montgomery Marches," Selma AL, March 7, 2015, https://obamawhitehouse.archives.gov/the-press-office/2015/03/07/remarks-president-50th-anniversary-selma-montgomery-marches.

13. "Women in U.S. Congress 2017," Center for American Women and Politics, http://www.cawp.rutgers.edu/women-us-congress-2017.

14. Anna Brown, "The Data on Women Leaders," Pew Research Center, March 17, 2017, http://www.pewsocialtrends.org/2017/03/17/the-data-on-women-leaders/.

15. Annalisa Merelli, "What's Killing America's New Mothers?," *Quartz*, October 29, 2017, https://qz.com/1108193/whats-killing-americas-new-mothers/.

16. Elizabeth Flock and Joshua Barajas, "They Reported Sexual Harassment. Then the Retaliation Began," PBS, March 1, 2018, https://www.pbs.org/newshour/nation/they-reported-sexual-harassment-then-the-retaliation-began.

17. Jones, Schmitt, and Wilson, "50 Years."

18. Raj Chetty and Nathaniel Hendren, "Race and Economic Opportunity in the United States," Equality of Opportunity Project, http://www.equality-of-opportunity.org/assets/documents/race_summary.pdf.

19. Linda Villarosa, "Why America's Black Mothers and Babies Are in a Life-or-Death Crisis," *New York Times Magazine*, April 11, 2018, https://www.nytimes.com/2018/04/11/magazine/black-mothers-babies-death-maternal-mortality.html.

20. Bryce Covert, "'We Are Human Beings': LGBTQ People Face Pervasive Workplace Discrimination amid GOP Inaction," *Rewire*, November 30, 2017, https://rewire.news/article/2017/11/30/human-beings-lgbtq-people-face-pervasive-workplace-discrimination-amid-gop-inaction/.

21. David Bier and Stuart Anderson, "White House Plan Bans 22 Million Legal Immigrants Over 5 Decades," CATO Institute, January 29, 2018, https://www.cato.org/blog/white-house-plan-bans-22-million-legal-immigrants-over-5-decades.

22. Linda R. Tropp and Dina G. Okamoto, "Why a U.S. Government Agency Deleted the Words 'Nation of Immigrants,'" *Guardian*, March 2, 2018, https://www.theguardian.com/commentisfree/2018/mar/02/america-nation -immigrants-uscis-deleted.

23. Sewell Chan, "14 Million Visitors to U.S. Face Social Media Screening," *New York Times*, March 31, 2018, https://www.nytimes.com/2018/03 /30/world/americas/travelers-visa-social-media.html.

24. David Leonhardt, "The American Dream, Quantified at Last," *New York Times*, December 11, 2016, https://www.nytimes.com/2016/12/08/opinion /the-american-dream-quantified-at-last.html.

25. Facundo Alvaredo, Lucas Chancel, Thomas Piketty, Emmanuel Saez, and Gabriel Zucman, World Inequality Report 2018 executive summary, December 14, 2017, http://wir2018.wid.world/files/download/wir2018-summary-english.pdf.

26. Bryan Caplan, "The World Might Be Better Off without College for Everyone," *Atlantic*, January/February 2018, https://www.theatlantic.com /magazine/archive/2018/01/whats-college-good-for/546590/.

27. Rana Foroohar, "How the Financing of Colleges May Lead to Disaster," *New York Review of Books*, October 13, 2016, https://www.nybooks.com /articles/2016/10/13/how-the-financing-of-colleges-may-lead-to-disaster/.

28. Diana C. Mutz, "Status Threat, Not Economic Hardship, Explains the 2016 Presidential Vote," Proceedings of the National Academy of Sciences, April 23, 2018, http://www.pnas.org/content/115/19/E4330.

29. William H. Frey, "The U.S. Will Become 'Minority White' in 2045, Census Projects," Brookings Institution, March 14, 2018, https://www.brookings .edu/blog/the-avenue/2018/03/14/the-us-will-become-minority-white-in -2045-census-projects/.

30. Remarks at the Presentation Ceremony for the Presidential Medal of Freedom, White House, January 19, 1989, https://www.reaganlibrary.gov /011989b.

31. Stephanie Saul, "Fewer Foreign Students Are Coming to U.S., Survey Shows," *New York Times*, November 13, 2017, https://www.nytimes.com/2017 /11/13/us/fewer-foreign-students-coming-to-us.html.

32. Walter Russell Mead, "The Big Shift: How American Democracy Fails Its Way to Success," *Foreign Affairs*, May/June 2018, https://www.foreignaffairs .com/articles/united-states/2018-04-16/big-shift.

33. Forfare Davis, "Collapsing at the Speed of Twitter," *National Review*, April 13, 2016, https://www.nationalreview.com/postmodern-conservative /social-media-twitter-politics-republic-virtue-individualism/.

34. Frances FitzGerald, *Fire in the Lake: The Vietnamese and the Americans in Vietnam* (New York: Back Bay Books, 2002), 8.

35. "The Woman Suffrage Crisis," *New York Times*, February 7, 1915, https://www .nytimes.com/1915/02/07/archives/the-woman-suffrage-crisis.html.

36. Economist/YouGov poll, April 2018, https://d25d2506sfb94s.cloudfront .net/cumulus_uploads/document/a849k68e2i/econTabReport.pdf.

37. Bahman Dehgan, ed., *America in Quotations* (Jefferson NC: McFarland and Company, 2003), 3.

38. "Measures Proposed to Amend the Constitution," https://www.senate .gov/reference/measures_proposed_to_amend_constitution.htm

39. James Fallows, "The Reinvention of America," *Atlantic*, May 2018, https://www.theatlantic.com/magazine/archive/2018/05/reinventing-america /556856/.

40. Edward Luce, *The Retreat of Western Liberalism* (New York: Atlantic Monthly Press, 2017), 190.

PART II

Conceptual Unifying Narratives

5

Can the United States Be One People?

GORDON S. WOOD

The United States is not a nation like other nations, and it never has been. There never has been any American ethnicity to back up the state called the United States, and there was no such distinctive ethnicity even in 1776, when the United States was created. Although the first paragraph of the Declaration of Independence in 1776 held out the promise of Americans becoming "one People," at the end of that document the members of the Continental Congress could only mutually pledge "to each other their lives, their fortunes, and their sacred honor."[1] There was nothing else but themselves they could dedicate themselves to—no patria, no fatherland, no nation as yet.

The American Revolution did not resemble modern colonial rebellions. It was not a consequence of two and half million people deciding in 1776 that they were a distinct ethnicity or nation that had to break away from the British Empire. The American Revolution was not like the Algerian separation from France in the 1960s or the Indian and Pakistani break from the British Empire in the 1940s. The Americans almost to the moment of declaring independence in 1776 considered themselves Englishmen, equal in every way to Englishmen in the metropolitan center, three thousand miles away. The rights they invoked in defense of themselves against the actions of the British government were English rights, such as no taxation without representation; they did not claim to have rights and privileges that were unique to them as Americans.

When the Continental Congress began to anticipate a break

from England in 1775, some of the delegates realized that to continue to talk of defending English rights was becoming embarrassing. So they decided to call these rights natural rights, but the rights were the same, good old English rights. It was a strange revolution, as some of the leaders realized, one that was undertaken on behalf of an uncorrupted English constitution, not in opposition to it.

Since the colonists had always thought of themselves as Englishmen or Britons, they were slow to think of themselves as "Americans." They shared no common history except as Britons. They shared no common historic institutions except the Crown and Parliament. Beyond their particular individual colony, their focus was on the mother country across the Atlantic, not on the other colonies. Until the Continental Congress met in Philadelphia in 1774, more of its members had been to London than had been to Philadelphia.[2]

During the colonial period the colonists did not call themselves Americans. It was the British officials in London who called the North American colonists "Americans." British officials were the ones who throughout the first half of the eighteenth century had imagined and feared the possibility of an independent America. In their minds they created America before the colonists did. It took the imperial crisis of 1765–76 to convince the colonists that they should have a separate destiny from the Englishmen at home. Only during that critical decade leading up to the Revolution did the colonists begin to refer to themselves as Americans.

There was certainly no real nation in 1776, not even a semblance of a real national government. Indeed, Americans had no experience being a nation or running a central government. "Prior to the revolution," John Jay later recalled, "we had little occasion to inquire or know much about national affairs. . . . War and peace, alliances and treaties, and commerce and navigation were conducted and regulated without our advice or controul."[3] With independence, the Americans' capacity to be a nation in a world of nations had to be learned on the fly.

In 1776 the thirteen separate states rather than the entity called the United States commanded people's loyalties. When Thomas

Jefferson talked about "my country" he meant Virginia.[4] Since there was no definition of national citizenship until the Fourteenth Amendment passed in the aftermath of the Civil War, people were citizens of a particular state, which is what made them citizens of the United States.

Americans at present are remarkably mobile and are apt to think of their home state as simply one administrative unit among many. Consequently, it is hard for Americans today to realize how emotionally important the states were to people of the early republic. Citizens of Virginia and Massachusetts had 150 years of provincial history to sustain their loyalty to their respective states. Against that experience the new United States could scarcely compete. The problem was similar to that of creating a sense of Europeanness today against the loyalty people feel toward their respective nations in Europe.

The initial central American authority was very weak. Indeed, the Continental Congress was not really a governmental body at all. John Adams called the Massachusetts delegation in the Continental Congress "our embassy."[5] The Congress was a delegation of embassies from each colony brought together by the exigency of events in 1774. It bore no resemblance to a legislature; instead, it was a gathering of separate, individual states to solve some common problems, similar, as its name indicates, to the Congress of Vienna of 1815. The Declaration of Independence, drawn up by the Continental Congress, was actually a declaration by "thirteen united States of America," proclaiming that as "Free and Independent States they have full power to levy war, conclude peace, contract alliances, establish commerce, and to do all the other things which independent States may of right do."[6] At the outset the United States of America had a literal plural meaning that was lost only with the consequences of the Civil War.

These independent states were very different from one another. It was their common language and their common English heritage that made them seem alike. Except for that common language and heritage, they were almost as different from one another as the eighteenth-century European states were from one another.

Puritan Massachusetts with its small farms and its pervasive sense of equality had very little in common with the aristocratic and slaveholding colony of Virginia, where 40 percent of the population was composed of African slaves.

Inevitably, these thirteen states, if they were to successfully fight Great Britain, the greatest power in the world, would have to have some sort of union. Hence they created the Articles of Confederation by signing a treaty among themselves. The confederation was not a state; it was a "league of friendship," a "confederation" of separate and independent states very similar to the present-day European Union.[7] Even getting the states to agree to this union was difficult, and it was not ratified by all the states until March 1781, three years after the Treaty of Alliance with France was signed and only six months before the Battle of Yorktown, which effectively ended the war. Consequently, during the war the states assumed powers that presumably belonged to only the Confederation Congress, including waging war, laying embargoes, and even in some cases carrying on separate diplomatic correspondence and negotiations abroad. Under such circumstances it was difficult for the collective entity called the United States to establish its character or reputation as a legitimate nation-state in the eyes of the world.

Initially, the country lacked nearly all the symbols of a real nation, one that had the respect of the civilized world. It had no flag, no great seal, no rites, no rituals, no ceremonies, no emblems of nationhood. The American commissioner in France, Silas Deane, was embarrassed that the Declaration of Independence arrived in France without proper authentication by a national seal, the use of seals, said Deane, being "a very ancient custom" in Europe. Unsure that it was dealing with a real nation-state, France in 1778 asked that "the thirteen United States of North America" individually ratify the commercial treaty and the military alliance that had been negotiated in Paris.

The ratification of the new Constitution in 1787–88 and the creation of a real national government gave many Americans a new sense of oneness. "'Tis done!" declared Dr. Benjamin Rush in July 1788. "We have become a nation." This was an exaggerated claim, to say the least, and most American leaders were well aware that America was not yet a nation and that it would not be easy to create one. Because of extensive immigration, America already seemed to have a diverse society. In addition to seven hundred thousand people of African descent and tens of thousands of native Indians, nearly all the peoples of Western Europe were present in the country. In the census of 1790 only 60 percent of the white population of well over three million was English in ancestry. The rest of the white population was composed of a variety of ethnicities. Nearly 9 percent was German, over 8 percent was Scots, 6 percent was Scots-Irish, nearly 4 percent was Irish, and over 3 percent was Dutch; the remainder was made up of French, Swedes, Spanish, and people of unknown ethnicity.

For eighteenth-century enlightened reformers, ethnic diversity and multiculturalism were not good things. Instead of emphasizing the multicultural variety of the different immigrants, reformers sought to accelerate the acculturation and assimilation of the many immigrants into one people, which, as the Massachusetts political and literary figure Fisher Ames pointed out, meant, "to use the modern jargon, nationalized."[8]

The revolutionary leaders' idea of a modern nation, shared by enlightened British, French, and German eighteenth-century reformers as well, was one that was composed of similar people, one that was not broken up by differences of language, ethnicity, religion, and local customs. Indeed, all the enlightened reformers in Europe were desperately trying to eliminate the peasant peculiarities and plebeian dialects that divided the people of their nation. Nothing was more frustrating to enlightened reformers on the eve of the French Revolution than the realization that the majority of Frenchmen did not speak French.

Sameness and uniformity among the people were desirable for any nation, but as Montesquieu had emphasized, they were especially desirable for a republic. The many state histories written in the aftermath of the Revolution were anything but celebrations of localism and the diversity of the nation. Indeed, declared David Ramsay, who wrote a history of his state of South Carolina, these local histories were testimonies to the American commitment to enlightened nationhood; they were designed, said Ramsay, to "wear away prejudices—rub off asperities and mould us into an homogeneous people."[9]

Homogeneous people! This is a phrase that separates Americans of today most decisively from that different, distant eighteenth-century world. Because we Americans today have survived as a nation for over two centuries, we can indulge ourselves with the luxury of celebrating our multicultural diversity. But two hundred years ago Americans were trying to create a nation from scratch and had no such luxury. They were desperately trying to make themselves one people and wondered whether America could ever be a real nation.

John Adams certainly had doubts that Americans could be a real nation. In America, he said, there was nothing like "the patria of the Romans, the Fatherland of the Dutch, or the Patrie of the French." All he saw in the country was an appalling diversity of religious denominations and ethnicities. At one point he counted at least twenty different religious sects in the United States, including some Protestants who believed in nothing. "We are such a Hotch potch of people," he concluded, "such an omnium gatherum of English, Irish, German, Dutch, Sweedes, French, &c. that it is difficult to give a name to the Country, characteristic of the people."[10]

It was indeed difficult, and Americans struggled with what to call their new country. Adams himself preferred "the simplest name of one syllable, like France or Spain, provided it was a bold & pleasant sound."[11] On the tercentenary celebration in 1792 of Columbus's discovery of America one patriot suggested "The United States of Columbia" as a name for the new republic. Poets ranging from the female black slave Phillis Wheatley to the Princeton graduate Philip Freneau saw the logic of the name and thus repeatedly referred to the nation as Columbia. With the same rhythm and number of syllables, Columbia could easily replace Britannia in new compositions set to the music of traditional English songs.

But Adams didn't like Columbia or Columbians. The words were unpleasant and sounded like gun, drum, trumpet, blunderbuss, and thunder. Besides, he didn't want to give "such wonderful honors to a bold navigator & successful adventurer." Columbus was celebrated enough. Adams thought Amerigo Vespucci, who was "a man of taste, sense & letters," better deserved the honor.[12]

So the name Columbia did not stick. Neither did Dr. Samuel Mitchill's suggestion that the new nation be called Fredonia and its people Fredonians. (It was the Marx Brothers who later made something of Freedonia.) Despite Mitchill's argument that "we cannot be national in feeling and in fact until we have a national name," the country's designation remained the "United States of America," with its people appropriating the name "Americans," which rightfully belonged to all the peoples of the New World.[13]

With the outbreak of a great war between Britain and France in the 1790s the United States became politically divided between the two parties of Federalists and Jeffersonian Republicans, and this division made the Americans' struggle to form a national identity all the more difficult. A large proportion of the population, most of whom were in New England, was deeply opposed to the Republican administration of Thomas Jefferson. Some New Englanders even began talking of taking their section out of the Union. Fear of the democratic passions unleashed by the party of Jeffersonian Republicans made many Federalists rethink and regret America's 1776 break from Great Britain. Amid a revolutionary world gone mad, Britain in 1809 seemed to be a bastion of stability, and in the words of Timothy Pickering, former Federalist secretary of state in the Washington and Adams administrations, it was "the country of our forefathers, and the country to which we are indebted for all the institutions held dear to freemen."[14]

Federalist newspapers and magazines now denied that there was any such thing as Americanness. Benjamin Rush in 1805 thought that most of the Federalists, who were, he said, "a majority of the old and wealthy *native* citizens," were "still Englishmen in their hearts." Indeed, Rush went so far as to admit that he had been wrong in 1788 in claiming that Americans had created a nation. They had, he now said, "no national character, and however much we may boast of it, there are very few true Americans in the United States."[15]

Many of the Federalists, including John Adams, couldn't help rooting for the former mother country in its titanic struggle with Napoleonic France. Because most Americans were anxiously trying to establish their identity as an independent people distinct from their British ancestors, the kinds of Anglophilic sentiments expressed by the Federalists were bound to be misinterpreted and used against them. The leader of the Federalists in the House of Representatives, Josiah Quincy, realized only too keenly the mistakes many of his colleagues were making in professing an emotional attachment to Great Britain. Not only did such professions do "little credit to their patriotism," but they did "infinitely less to their judgment. The truth is," he said in 1812, "the British look upon us as a *foreign nation*, and we must look upon them in the same light."[16]

Although the War of 1812 with Great Britain ended in a draw, most Americans thought it had been a great victory. The United States, once thought to be so fragile that it would soon fall apart, emerged from the war with a new sense of strength and unity. The people, observed the Republican secretary of the treasury, Albert Gallatin, in 1815, "are more American; they feel and act more as a nation; and I hope that the permanency of the Union is thereby better secured."[17] The war, which Americans called a second American revolution, seemed to vindicate the Americans' bold experiment in democracy. The Federalists were completely discredited, and the new republic gained a self-confidence that it had never possessed before.

Yet the question remained how to fill out and develop this new sense of nationhood. Hezekiah Niles, the most important journalist of the early nineteenth century, was keen to establish "a NATIONAL CHARACTER" for Americans. Despite the victory over Britain in the War of 1812, Niles knew that eliminating the old English habits of mind was essential to establishing that national character. If we were to have a new nation, Niles declared in a public appeal in 1817 addressed to the two former Republican presidents, Thomas Jefferson and James Madison, we needed new principles, new ideas, new ways of thinking. "We seek a new revolution, not less important, perhaps, in its consequences than that of 1776—a revolution in letters, a shaking off of the fetters of the mind." To do this, he said, "we must begin with the establishment of first principles," principles that were best found in Jefferson's Declaration of Independence. Thus the Declaration "shall be the base of all the rest—the *common reference* in cases of doubt and difficulty."[18]

It may have been this extraordinary celebration of the Declaration of Independence that helped convince Jefferson that his writing of the Declaration should be listed first among the three great achievements of his life that he wanted engraved on his tombstone. It is not surprising that he soon came to believe that the desk on which he had written the Declaration would become a sacred relic.

Lincoln probably never read Niles's 1817 public appeal to Jefferson, but he had the same insight. When he declared in 1858 "all honor to Jefferson," he paid homage to the one Founder who he knew could explain why the United States was one nation and why so many lives had to be sacrificed to maintain that one nation. Lincoln knew what the Revolution had been about and what it implied not just for Americans but for all humanity— because Jefferson had told him so. The United States was a new republican nation alone in a world of monarchies, especially alone since the failure of all the republican revolutions of 1848; it was a grand experiment in self-government, conceived in liberty and dedicated to the proposition that all men are created equal.

Half the American people, said Lincoln in 1858, had no direct blood connection to the Founders of the nation. These German, Irish, French, and Scandinavian citizens had come from Europe themselves, or their ancestors had, and they had settled in America, "finding themselves our equals in all things." Although these immigrants may have had no actual connection in blood with the revolutionary generation that could make them feel part of the rest of the nation, they had, said Lincoln, "that old Declaration of Independence," with its expression of the moral principle of equality, to draw upon. This moral principle, which was "applicable to all men and all times," made all these different peoples one with the Founders, "as though they were blood of the blood and flesh of the flesh of the men who wrote that Declaration." This emphasis on liberty and equality, he said, was "the electric cord . . . that links the hearts of patriotic and liberty-loving men together, that will link those patriotic hearts as long as the love of freedom exists in the minds of men throughout the world."[19]

In Jefferson's Declaration Lincoln found a solution to the great problem of American identity: how the great variety of individuals in America, with all their diverse ethnicities, races, and religions, could be brought together into one nation. As Lincoln grasped better than anyone ever has, the Revolution and its Declaration of Independence offered Americans a set of beliefs that through the generations have supplied a bond that holds together the most diverse nation that history has ever known. Since now the whole world is in the United States, nothing but the ideals coming out of the Revolution can turn such an assortment of different individuals into the "one people" that the Declaration says we are. To be an American is not to be someone but to believe in something. And of that something most important is the belief that all men are created equal.

The idea of equality is the most radical and most powerful ideological force that the Revolution unleashed. It became and remains what Herman Melville called "the great God absolute! The centre and circumference of all democracy!" This "Spirit of Equality," said Melville, did not just cull the "selectest champions from the kingly commons"; more important, it spread "one royal mantle of humanity" over all Americans and bestowed "democratic dignity" on even "the arm that wields a pick or drives a spike."[20] This powerful sense of equality is still alive and well in America, and despite all of its disturbing and unsettling consequences, it is what makes us one people.

Notes

1. Declaration of Independence, in *The Constitution of the United States and the Declaration of Independence* (National Constitution Center, 2009), 35, 39.

2. John M. Murrin, "A Roof without Walls: The Dilemma of American Politics," in *Beyond Confederation: The Origins of the Constitution and American National Identity*, ed. Richard Beeman et al. (Chapel Hill: University of North Carolina Press, 1987), 340.

3. David M. Golove and Daniel J. Hulsebosch, "A Civilized Nation: The Early American Constitution, the Law of Nations, and the Pursuit of International Recognition," *New York University Law Review* 85 (2010): 961.

4. See Ronald L. Hatzenbuehler, *"I Tremble for My Country": Thomas Jefferson and the Virginia Gentry* (Gainesville: University Press of Florida, 2006).

5. John Adams to Abigail Adams, September 18, 1774, in *Adams Family Correspondence*, ed. L. H. Butterfield et al. (Cambridge MA: Harvard University Press, 1963), 1:158.

6. Declaration of Independence, 38–39.

7. Articles of Confederation, in *Colonies to Nation, 1763–1789: A Documentary History of the American Revolution*, ed. Jack P. Greene (New York: W. W. Norton, 1967), 428–35.

8. Fisher Ames, "Falkland III, 10 Feb. 1801," in *Works of Fisher Ames* (1854), ed. W. B. Allen (Indianapolis: Liberty Fund, 1983), 1:216.

9. David Ramsay to John Eliot, August 11, 1792, in *David Ramsey, 1749–1815: Selections from His Writings*, ed. Robert L. Brunhouse, American Philosophical Society, n.s. 55, pt. 4 (1965): 133.

10. John Adams to William Tudor, February 25, 1800, in *John Adams: Writings from the New Nation*, ed. Gordon S. Wood (New York, 2016), 388–89.

11. Adams to Tudor, February 25, 1800, 388–89.

12. Claudia L. Bushman, *America Discovers Columbus: How an Italian Explorer Became an American Hero* (Hanover NH, 1992), 41–51; Adams to Tudor, February 25, 1800, 389.

13. Alan David Aberbach, *In Search of an American Identity: Samuel Latham Mitchill, Jeffersonian Nationalist* (New York, 1988), 154–56.

14. Henry Adams, ed., *Documents Relating to New England Federalism, 1800–1815* (Boston, 1877), 389.

15. Benjamin Rush to John Adams, June 29 and August 14, 1805, in *The Spur of Fame: Dialogues of John Adams and Benjamin Rush, 1805–1813*, ed. John A. Schutz and Douglass Adair (San Marino CA: Huntington Library, 1966), 28, 31.

16. Bradford Perkins, *Prologue to War* (Berkeley: University of California Press, 1961), 61.

17. Albert Gallatin to Matthew Lyon, May 7, 1816, in *The Writings of Albert Gallatin*, ed. Henry Adams (Philadelphia, 1879), 2:700.

18. Hezekiah Niles to Thomas Jefferson and James Madison, in *The Papers of Thomas Jefferson: Retirement Series*, ed. J. Jefferson Looney et al. (Princeton NJ: Princeton University Press, 2015), 12:162.

19. Abraham Lincoln to Henry L. Pierce and others, April 6, 1859, in *Abraham Lincoln, Speeches and Writings, 1832–1865*, ed Don E. Fehrenbacher (New York, 1974), 2:19; Lincoln, speech given in Chicago, July 19, 1858, in Fehrenbacher, *Abraham Lincoln*, 1:456.

20. Herman Melville, *Moby-Dick* (1851), ed. Harrison Hayford and Hershel Parker (New York, 1967), chap. 26, 104–5.

6

Holding Ourselves Together

JOHN C. DANFORTH

The great American purpose is, as it has been from our beginning, to hold together in one nation a diverse and often contentious people. So broadly do we embrace this purpose that we proclaim it in our motto, and we commit our loyalty to it with our hands over our hearts. Our motto, *e pluribus unum*, states that while we are of different interests and origins, we are one people. We pledge our allegiance to one nation, indivisible. Aspiring to realize this purpose and to progress toward it, politically and socially, defines our identity and is a source of our pride. Becoming in reality one united people always has been and will remain a work in progress, requiring a well-structured and effectively functioning government and, most importantly, drawing on the goodness of the American people.

In our early history, the work of holding ourselves together was mostly political. We began as a confederation of sovereign states, each able to go its own way, but that quickly proved inadequate to the task of providing for the common defense and promoting the general welfare, so we created a new constitution "in order to form a more perfect union." Still, the question of whether we were essentially one nation, the United States, or a collection of separate states remained open until it was resolved by the Civil War. We can imagine Robert E. Lee pacing the halls of his Virginia mansion, debating whether his primary allegiance was to the federal government or his state, but we cannot imagine that he could have resolved the question in favor of Virginia. Today, it seems inconceivable that the matter warranted a second thought.

The more difficult challenge before the Constitutional Convention, and the one that persists today, was not that of binding together the several states but that of holding together in one nation a people of competing political and economic interests. How to do this was James Madison's great gift to America. Madison was a realist who knew that we would always have competing interests, what he called "factions," and he designed a structure of government that would allow factions to compete against one another, thereby guarding against what he feared most, the tyranny of the majority. Congress was to be the branch of government where public policy was to be debated and made, and the two houses of Congress were to represent our competing interests. Our capacity to hold ourselves together given our opposing factions would depend on the working of Congress, a functioning U.S. Senate and a functioning House of Representatives. In the past decade, the Senate has become dysfunctional.

The normal process of a functioning Senate is called the "regular order," and it reflects what schoolchildren learn about how a bill becomes a law. Bills are supposed to go through hearings and amendments in committee, then debate and amendments on the floor. In the past decade, the regular order has been abandoned as bills are drafted by the leadership of the majority party with no minority input or support. The most consequential legislation of the decade, Obamacare and tax reform, received no participation from the minority. During the same decade, the filibuster evolved from the exception to the rule, so a disciplined minority party has been able to block or delay confirmation of presidential nominees as well as legislation. Few bills become laws, and the country lurches from crisis to crisis with periodic threats that if the Senate doesn't act, it will shut down the government. Historically, the Senate has been known as "the world's greatest deliberative body." That is hardly the case today.

In part, blame for this dysfunction lies with the Senate itself. Its schedule, the demands of constant travel for fund-raising, and the cost of living in Washington mean that families are often absent, and members know one another as politicians, not as friends. Moreover, hyperpartisanship works against the kind of open communication that makes for collegiality. One senator told me that members are wary of using humor for fear that whatever they say is being recorded secretly for use in a future campaign.

But the greater blame lies not with a few people in Washington but with us, the American people. Often we hear the complaint that politicians don't listen. That is the opposite of the truth. They listen, perhaps to a fault. They conduct opinion polls and convene focus groups. They make countless public appearances. If they don't listen, they don't get elected, and they surely care about getting elected. The problem isn't that they don't listen, it's what they hear. And what they hear from the base of each party, from the activists who speak out, contribute money, and vote in primary elections, is, "Don't compromise. Don't give an inch. If you dare work with the other party, you will not be our nominee." The pressure is toward the poles, and there is no overlap between the two parties. The political center has collapsed.

The framers of our Constitution designed a structure that would require compromise, which would result from bringing the competing factions together in one place. Without compromise, the Senate would not serve its intended purpose as a place to work out our differences. It would not play its part in holding America together. It would amount to little more than what it has now become, a place for making speeches.

• • •

Restoring a functioning constitutional structure that can accommodate our competing factions is a necessary but not the only condition for holding America together. Beyond a functioning government, there is work for all of us to do in addressing the persistent and developing societal conditions that separate us. These are our differences of race, religion, national origin, and gender and, recently, our physical isolation from one another, facilitated by modern communication and transportation.

The Constitution, which gave us the means of resolving our factional differences, perpetrated the most heinous cause of our division by protecting the institution of slavery. In 1865 the Thirteenth Amendment abolished slavery, but legal discrimination by race persisted with the enactment of Jim Crow laws in the South. The notion that racial segregation could be consistent with equality remained the law until the Supreme Court decided *Brown v. Board of Education* in 1954. Segregation in the private sector remained lawful until prohibited in employment and public accommodations by the Civil Rights Act of 1964. Even where not a formal policy, separation by race was the norm for much of America until well after the middle of the twentieth century. From elementary school through graduation from college in 1958, I never had an African American classmate.

Much for the good has happened in the last half century, brought about both by the acts of government and by the work of good people such as my nephew Donald Danforth III and my daughter Mary Stillman, who have founded schools that provide quality education to predominantly African American populations. Still, in our cities, many black Americans live in poorer sections of town, lack access to good schools, and fall behind in every economic measurement. As events in Ferguson, Missouri, and the Black Lives Matter movement teach us, many black Americans believe that they are the targets of discriminatory, sometimes brutal, treatment by the police.

And it's not only African Americans who feel estranged from the "system." In *Hillbilly Elegy*, J. D. Vance has made the case that whites with their roots in Appalachia feel abused and isolated from the rest of America.

Besides race, Americans have been divided by religion, national origin, and gender. Virulent anti-Catholicism, which reached its peak with the No Nothing Party of the mid-nineteenth century, diminished, and the evil of antisemitism was exposed as we learned of the Holocaust. But reaction to 9/11 brought outbreaks of Islamophobia that were fanned by the words and actions of President Donald Trump. In recent times, conservative Christians have insisted that governmental efforts to coerce their support of abortion and same-sex marriage amount to a war on their religious practices. The anti-immigrant fervor of the nineteenth century has gained new life as "Build the Wall!" has become the rallying cry for the right wing. Hispanics who know no other country than ours live in fear that they will be rounded up for deportation.

With regard to gender, women, once denied the vote, now hold countless positions in government and business. Title IX of the Education Amendments Act of 1972 barred sex discrimination in education. Still, many women have discovered that the glass ceiling persists, and lurid stories of workplace harassment show that employment can lead to abuse instead of equality. The widespread accessibility of pornography to an extent unimagined a half century ago has created a culture that does worse than marginalize women, it degrades them.

The one area where America is clearly more inclusive than in the past is sexual orientation. Relationships that many had thought repugnant are now legally protected and increasingly accepted.

With regard to race, religion, national origin, and gender, the sources of our divisions have mutated over time, and some, such as legal segregation, have disappeared. Our mission of holding together a diverse people in one indivisible nation has been a work in progress. Progress has been uneven and certainly incomplete, but in general it has been real. But when we shift our focus from demographics to individuals we see that the opposite is the case. We have become more separated from our neighbors, a condition David Brooks has called "the atomization of society." Harvard's Robert Putnam described the phenomenon in his famous book, *Bowling Alone*. Putnam showed that beginning in the last third of the twentieth century we evolved from a nation of joiners to a nation of isolated individuals. Instead of belonging to bowling leagues, we go bowling alone. The more interconnected we become by the internet and highways, the more separated we become from each other. We don't have to venture out to places where we meet colleagues and neighbors. We can sit alone in front of our computers and TVs. We can work at home, entertain ourselves at home, and educate our children at home. Texting can replace face-to-face meetings. When we do go out, we can still be by ourselves, alone behind the wheels of our cars. Historic creators of social capital—churches, service organizations, the PTA—have declined in significance.

Even when we are with others, we can retain our separation from most of society. Bill Bishop pointed this out in his book *The Big Sort*. The automobile has enabled us to live far from work and in communities with people who look, think, and vote just like us.

• • •

As holding together a diverse and often contentious people in one indivisible nation is our great American purpose, what can we the people do to advance that purpose? Here are some suggestions that would call on us as citizens to take personal responsibility for our country. None of these suggestions can be satisfied by delegating our responsibility to some external power or hoping that a new government program by itself will solve our problems for us.

First, with regard to our broken political system, let's mend it. Let's make government what the framers of the Constitution intended it to be, a place for holding together contending factions. To do this, many more Americans will have to be much more active in politics. They will have to show up at town hall meetings, communicate with office holders, and, above all, vote in primary elections. And they will have to deliver a message quite different from the uncompromising threats made by the activist extremes of the parties. They must say that there is something much more important than any policy they might support. They must insist simply on government that works. In America, government that works requires compromise. Compromise is essential if government is to fulfill its responsibility of holding us together.

For citizens to insist on compromise will require a generosity of spirit now uncommon in our political discourse, particularly on cable news networks. People who disagree with us are not our enemies; they simply have different opinions. For many of us, a generosity of spirit will take a change of heart. In 2016 60 percent of Republicans and 63 percent of Democrats said that they wanted their daughters to marry someone of the same party.[1] In 2017 33 percent of college students said they had blocked or "unfriended" someone on social media because of the presidential election.[2] So here is a small idea: make it a point to greet people of opposing political opinions by saying, "I am your friend."

A couple of additional suggestions:

1. Welcome diverse opinions, especially on college campuses where controversial speakers are sometimes shouted down.

2. Change the channel or read a different website when what you see whips you into a frenzy of anger.

Second, with regard to societal divisions, let's mend them as well, starting by being aware that some of our fellow Americans believe that they do not have a full stake in our country. Healing demographic divisions has historically involved government action and will continue to do so, for example, by increasing minority representation in law enforcement. Action by government depends on the consent of the governed and has often triggered backlash, especially when the issue is racial justice. Again, let's be generous of spirit. And much healing work can happen outside government. Citizens can take their own initiative by participating in efforts that better integrate minorities into American life, for example, by supporting educational enrichment programs for underserved populations.

And of great importance, let's be alert that some politicians seek to advance themselves by dividing us along ethnic or class lines. The word for them is "demagogues." It is up to us to call out the demagogues and to make it our business to ensure that their tactics backfire.

Third, with regard to the individualistic isolation that turns us from being a people into an assortment of inwardly directed persons, let's restore our civil society, those community organizations that bring us together. For many of us, this will mean getting out of the comfort zone of our self-imposed separation, joining groups, and being with others. In their book *American Grace*, Robert Putnam and David Campbell describe the correlation between membership in a religious congregation and participating in other organizations such as the Rotary and the PTA. They state that the relationship is independent of theology, preaching, and liturgy and suggest that it is causal. If they are correct, a good place to start bringing together an atomized society would be to join a house of worship.

• • •

Creating one nation out of many parts is America's national purpose and our ongoing project. Throughout our history, much of our progress has come by writing a constitution and enacting laws. Increasingly, responsibility for our progress rests on all of us as Americans. It will be our work to demand a functioning government where compromise is the norm, to integrate all our people into one indivisible nation, and to incorporate separated individuals into the wholeness of community.

Notes

1. Lynn Vavreck, "A Measure of Identity: Are You Wedded to Your Party?," *New York Times*, January 31, 2017, https://www.nytimes.com/2017/01/31/upshot/are-you-married-to-your-party.html.

2. "2017 Survey of America's College Students," Panetta Institute for Public Policy, May 2017, 9, http://www.panettainstitute.org/wp-content/uploads/Youth-Civic-Engagement-Survey-Report-2017-new.pdf.

7

Society and Service

JIM BANKS

People often complain of an America run by elites of wealth and power. There is certainly some truth to this viewpoint, but it fails to provide the entire picture. Our nation's virtue is steeped in the foundational principle of governance "of the people, by the people, and for the people." This indispensable component of our country's DNA largely remains intact, and its perseverance through generations has helped the United States grow into the greatest nation in world history. Yet today it is unraveling and under attack.

As a son of a factory worker and a nursing home cook, I arrived in Washington DC from a background of neither wealth nor power. My passion for civic engagement brought me to serve in our nation's capital. I find myself in Congress at a unique time in our history, a time when public service is being derided as either useless or fake and when, at times, society feels as if it is breaking apart at the seams. If we are to hope for a future amid the loss of trust in our political system, it is civic participation in and out of government, *by the people,* that must remain and be reinvigorated. This critically includes the role that people with regular backgrounds like my own play in serving others throughout all of society: in the military, faith communities, businesses, social groups, and elsewhere. Civic participation can mend our political and societal wounds in these pressing times.

My Background

While my father's side of the family originally came from the same Appalachian area in southeast Kentucky that J. D. Vance discusses in his book *Hillbilly Elegy*, I was born and raised in Columbia City,

Indiana, a small town of around five thousand people when I was born.[1] Raised in the middle of America's heartland, I am proud to still call it my home as I raise another generation of Bankses. For the first few years of my life, I grew up in a trailer park not far from where my father worked long, hard hours at an automotive plant and my mom cooked for patients at a nursing home. My parents may not have possessed much, but they cared a great deal for me and my younger brothers. Their "American Dream" was that my brothers and I would grow up with better potential and opportunities than they had, and they certainly gave all three of us a shot at just that.

In high school I had the opportunity to participate on the debate team. After teaming up with my debate partner, Joe, I became an Indiana high school state debate champion. Through this experience, I first learned about the good that can come to society through civil discourse and sound arguments pleaded passionately. Later, as the first in my family to go to college, I took my first step into civic participation by joining College Republicans and volunteering for political campaigns. I came to directly see what a difference political engagement can make, and, most of all, I benefited from meeting my wife during that time. After graduating, I worked briefly at Focus on the Family and then decided to work in business, where I eventually found opportunities in the commercial real estate and construction industries in northeast Indiana.

When I was growing up, our family was not exactly a political family, and politicians usually were not spoken of favorably in our working-class home. So it came as a surprise to many that I ascended through the ranks of local, state, and national politics in a span of about ten years. The uniqueness of our political system allowed me to do just that with a dream and inspiration to serve.

Shortly before I was thirty years old, I had the opportunity to serve in a leadership role in my home county's local Republican Party, mostly because no one else wanted to be the county chairman. I was later elected to serve as a member of the County Council, gaining a great perspective on local government and the importance of government that is closest to the people. A few years later, when my childhood dermatologist decided to retire after serving for over a decade, I was elected to serve as a state senator in the Indiana General Assembly. Around that time, I followed a desire I had since childhood: to serve in the military. Both of my grandfathers and one of my brothers had served, so it was a passion of mine to contribute to our country in a similar way.

After joining the U.S. Navy Reserve, I was quickly deployed to Afghanistan, which was one of the most challenging yet rewarding experiences of my life. Thankfully, Indiana law allows elected officials to take a temporary leave of absence for active military duty. While I served overseas, my wife, Amanda, was elected to take my place during my deployment, in the process proving that she is superhuman by simultaneously serving as a state senator and taking care of our three very young daughters. Every day since I returned from my deployment, I have been told how much better a job my wife did as state senator than me, and I do not doubt it. I had always heard of the challenges military spouses face while their loved ones are away, and as I watched Amanda excel in her dual roles, I personally saw just how central their role is to our national security.

Almost as soon as I returned from Afghanistan, my predecessor in the U.S. House of Representatives announced his bid for Indiana's open U.S. Senate seat. I felt called to run for the newly vacant House seat, to be a voice for my fellow Hoosiers of northeast Indiana, advocate on their behalf, and give back to my community and country in a new way. This was a chance to fight to rebuild the military, protect economic opportunity and the American dream, and stand up for the most defenseless in our nation—the unborn. Because of the generous support of the citizens of the Third District, I have been representing northeast Indiana in Congress since January 2017. Only in America can someone from a very ordinary background like mine ascend to a national leadership role in the U.S. House of Representatives. At the same time, I believe we need to do more to make sure that our future leaders are afforded the same ability and opportunity and that they are inspired to do so in the first place.

Public Discourse

Throughout my time in public service, I have seen the crucial importance of civil public discourse, and I believe the disintegration of civility in our national conversation is directly related to inspiring new generations of leaders to serve. The way people communicate with one another can make a big difference, for better or worse. We are so fortunate that in America we can almost always settle disputes without the barrel of a gun or a back-door bribe. Many in a place like Vladimir Putin's Russia would love to have that good fortune, that simple but hard-won element of prosperity that comes with the rule of law. Just ask Bill Browder or Sergei Magnitsky's family, for instance.[2] But we are struggling, in a lesser yet still very significant way, with the civility of our public discourse.

Our country has had unfriendly political debates; to a large degree, they are nothing new. Tensions flared between Adams and Jefferson, who each had impassioned views on the direction for the fledgling nation.[3] Engaging in debates on issues is essential to the American way. But those participating in debates have usually been open to hearing what the other side has to say. Today we seem to have reached a whole new level of anger. In many instances, open dialogue or debate is ignored as each side resorts to angry monologues to like-minded audiences. This may not be hostility, but it is certainly not hospitality. And it prompts the question: Can society function somewhere in between?

With the invention of Twitter, the art of debate has been boiled down to 280 characters—quick, short retorts—instead of impassioned, thoughtful dialogue. Social media has provided an incredible opportunity to bridge the divide between the public and public servants. There have been opportunities to engage in meaningful discussion with citizens in real time like never before. Yet much of my timeline on Twitter consists of anonymous tweets like, "Hey Jim, just in case you haven't been told by today, you suck" or "LOL, you're so stupid Banks." While I am not allergic to criticism and welcome critical feedback, these interactions make me wonder how much these individuals engage with their fellow citizens. How much has anyone benefited by any similar simple one-liners?

We have to wonder if the mask of anonymity disrupts most of the good that might come from such activity. It is one thing to stand in front of someone and have the courage to debate them, along with the mutual respect that is usually granted in personal interaction. It is entirely different to cowardly stir the pot because no one can know who did it, and all for what gain? Arthur Brooks, the president of the American Enterprise Institute, has decried just how toxic anonymous posting is and how internet "trolling" is not adding any value to the conversation.[4]

Social media entrepreneurs themselves are questioning the utility of the very platforms they created and fostered. Former Twitter CEO Evan Williams remarked, "I thought once everybody could speak freely and exchange information and ideas, the world is automatically going to be a better place. I was wrong about that."[5] Facebook's first president, Sean Parker, stated, "I don't know if I really understood the consequences of what I was saying. Because of the unintended consequences of a network . . . of a billion or two people, it literally changes your relationship with society and with each other."[6] And former Facebook VP Chamath Palihapitiya worried, "I think we have created tools that are ripping apart the social fabric of how society works. . . . The short-term, dopamine-driven feedback loops we've created are destroying how society works. . . . No civil discourse, no cooperation; misinformation, mistruth."[7]

These platforms are great tools in many ways, and I use them all the time. However, they are not always the tools for meaningful discussion as originally intended. Interaction between people in a real-life setting cannot be captured or mimicked by these platforms. The more someone communicates behind a screen, the less they are concerned with interpersonal diplomacy and the more they are inclined to engage in verbal attacks. Sadly, we even see international affairs playing out over Twitter instead of more appropriate platforms. President Trump, for instance, tweeted, "Why would Kim Jong-un insult me by calling me 'old,' when I would NEVER call him 'short and fat?'"

Civil discourse must begin with those that society entrusts most to model civility.

The right to free speech is fundamental and can never go away; it is one of the most essential protections of any government worth having. But preserving a culture of civility is critical on a nongovernmental level, as a society. Harvard Business School professor David Moss, in his book *Democracy: A Case Study*, discusses how political conflict is in fact very good and healthy; it is part of the lifeblood of a flourishing democratic republic. This is only the case, though, *if* it is constructive. Effective solutions are built in large part directly because of debate and deliberation. Our entire country has been built on such public discourse, from the debates on whether and when we should break from Great Britain, to what the Constitution would include, to what wars we should wage.[8]

Moss asserts that we must ask ourselves today if we can argue, debate, oppose, and advocate our stances constructively, or if we will allow such divides to burn the bridges to our fellow countrymen. *Productive* tension, as he calls it, requires us to maintain a shared faith in our political system and the way our society is constructed at large—a faith in the unity of one country that is made up of differing opinions. We can succeed while disagreeing on many things. But this works only if we do not give up on the peaceable manner of discourse, and only if we do not give up on public discourse and public service altogether.[9]

Societal Breakdown

The disconnect and hostility we see amid ever-increasing digital "connectivity" is symptomatic of a larger societal breakdown across our country. We hear of books like *Bowling Alone*, and we see that things are not how they used to be. Our participation in everything from bowling leagues to Rotary Clubs to faith communities has fallen drastically.[10] Instead of teasing a friend for getting a 7/10 split on the bowling lane, we send a mudslinging Twitter comment behind the anonymity of the computer screen. Instead of talking heads in the media talking to each other, they talk past each other. Instead of families staying together, they break apart. Instead of those with different political views having a beer together, they unfriend each other on Facebook. And instead of children being the priority in education, schools are pulled into the political battles of adults.

People do not find the sense of belonging they once did. Through my time working in the Indiana Senate and in Congress to help our nation's veterans, I have seen a vivid example of the dire effects of social decay. I came across the book *Tribe* by wartime journalist Sebastian Junger, whose hypothesis on post-traumatic stress disorder (PTSD), even if disagreed with, must be considered. He asserts that much of the difficulties faced by veterans when they return home is due to no longer being part of the tight-knit community forged between their fellow brothers and sisters in arms. They go from having the camaraderie and support system of a platoon facing tragedy and triumph together to isolation back home. Junger believes that much of PTSD is directly caused by this jarring reentrance into a disconnected society.[11]

Junger has perhaps revealed a big piece of the puzzle, although it is difficult to measure that piece empirically. At the very least, we know that as society has broken down, rates of PTSD have risen. Every single day, twenty veterans die by suicide. This tragedy motivated my Veterans Crisis Line Study Act legislation, which would strengthen this resource for veterans in times of need. It seeks to ensure that those veterans who are struggling can find the mental health assistance they need. However, until society at large is healed, we will still have a great need for improvement.

Many blame society's ills on insufficient government programs in one area or another. The belief that government can cure everything is strongest inside the Washington Beltway. Many there think that what happens in Congress or the White House is real America. They think that these are the places where we can find our way and fix everything. But Washington is not real America. Real America is a family at the dinner table. Real America is the Rotary Club. Real America is the Boy Scouts. And even these are crumbling, in part due to the increase of government involvement in our daily lives. It is important to recognize that as social cohesion has plummeted, government spending has skyrocketed. In *The Fractured Republic*, Yuval Levin writes about how government centralization of everything has helped tear apart the intermediary levels of society that exist between the level of the individual and the level of the entire nation. The government has helped produce the social ills that so many believe it is uniquely capable of curing.[12]

As citizens in real America experience society's breakdown, some increasingly accept the false claim that the federal government can actually fix everything. They then become disappointed when it cannot do the job on its own. On the other hand, some not only accept this reality to begin with but view any involvement in politics as cancerous. Today, it is almost doctrine to some that if one is "in the swamp," one is necessarily "of the swamp." Occupations in public service are denigrated to the extent that many feel it is so toxic that they do not even want to participate. Some simply do not want to be hired to be told by their opposing party, their colleagues, the media, and their fellow citizens that there is no single good act they can do regardless of their efforts. Such antipathy toward sincere attempts to resolve our crises will become a self-fulfilling prophecy that prevents us from deploying an essential part of the solution.

Public Service

Part of the healing for society must come from a new generation of young people who are willing to take part in public service for the good of those they serve. At the very least, those with goodwill and a certain level of ability must be ready to counteract those who lack these qualities. The upcoming generation can do the job of getting the government out of the way, reducing its scope, and giving back the reins to state and local governments and to families and individuals. Additionally, they can contribute real change in the areas that only government can reach, especially national defense. Instead of throwing textual bombs, they can lay bricks, building upon the firm foundation our Founders set for us to meet the challenges we would face. Government can never be the whole solution for society, but a lack of good government will inevitably be one of its most fatal flaws. Ultimately, America's future cannot be built upon the exodus of an entire generation from faithful and skilled public service.

One of my inspirations in public service is a man from the other side of the aisle, President John F. Kennedy. Shortly after becoming president, he recorded some of his thoughts in preparation for one day writing his memoirs, a book that ultimately the nation was robbed of seeing published. He demonstrated that politics has always been an object of scorn in society, but it is a component that is necessary and essential. His perspective helped convince me of the good that I might be able to contribute in Congress. He stated:

> In a sense, it is important and desirable that people feel this way about politics and politicians in a free society. A politician's power may be great, and with this power goes the necessity of checking it. But the fact remains that politics has become one of our most abused and neglected professions. It ranks low on the occupational list of a large share of the American population. Yet it is this profession which makes the great decisions of war and peace, prosperity and recession, the decision whether we look to the future or the past. . . . It seems to me that governmental service is the way to translate . . . interest into action. . . . Winston Churchill once said, "Democracy is the worst form of government except for all of the other systems that have been tried." It is certainly the most demanding; it requires more from us all than any other system. The magic of politics is not the panoply of office. It is playing a small role in determining whether, in . . . Faulkner's words, "freedom will not only endure, but also prevail."[13]

Kennedy was right. There is ample reason to always be skeptical of politicians. A presidential predecessor and the father of the Constitution, James Madison, once said, "All men having power ought to be distrusted to a certain degree."[14] Yet a healthy dose of skepticism ought to be accompanied by a healthy dose of trust in what Churchill understood as the best of these flawed systems. And there ought to be a sense of duty to take part in its governance. America can only thrive with good, young individuals with fresh perspectives being attracted to public service on every level—local, state, and federal.

We need a renewed spirit of public service that recognizes the worth in fighting to preserve the structure that preserves our freedom. It is not a service driven by a faith in government to solve all things. It is a faith in the inalienable rights of life, liberty, and the pursuit of happiness and in the need for a government that recognizes these rights and its own inability to solve all societal problems. Without a constant fight to keep this type of government going, we will most assuredly see a slide away from freedom. Vladimir Putin and Xi Jinping want to convince the world, and especially their own people, that democratic republican government cannot succeed. We must have a generation of young people who prove them wrong time and again. As society breaks down, we need young people who do not fear that the worst is inevitable but who have the will and grit to weather this storm as we have every other.

This need for the participation of young people is needed in the military as well, for our freedoms are only as secure as they are defended. After my grandparents' generation sent most of their young, able-bodied men to the front lines in World War II, many in the current generation are not even eligible to serve. The most recent estimates from the Heritage Foundation indicate that only 29 percent of Americans between ages seventeen and twenty-four qualify. The reasons range from avoidable health problems to drug use to insufficient education. This is a military readiness crisis for our country.[15] Service in the military is service to something bigger than oneself, and we should encourage our young people, when possible, to take that step. There will always be threats to our freedom, and we need those with youthful vigor to stand up to them and preserve previously hard-fought victories.

Civility in Public Service

Public service alone is not enough; quality of service is vital. We see the lack of civility too regularly in our nation's capital. Take, for example, former Senate Majority Leader Harry Reid, who outright slandered the Republican presidential candidate Mitt Romney on the eve of the 2012 election. He took to the Senate floor to make the completely unsubstantiated claim that Romney had not paid his taxes. PolitiFact rated this claim "completely false." Senator Reid's response when questioned about it was, "Well, they can call it whatever they want. Romney didn't win, did he?"[16] That is not leadership; it is defamatory propaganda, yet Reid's example is one of so many we can choose from. More and more, the public discounts everyone in public service due to the distortions of some like Reid. Our leaders must do more to preserve our institutions of government and public service by striving toward civility and restoring the public's trust.

Society seems to be at a crossroads at this unique point in time. Every day is a chance to foster the constructive dialogue our future prosperity requires. As our public institutions break down in every sector—whether it is the government, religion, media, family, or education—we should all seek to do what we can to avoid contributing to that decay. One of the first things I did when I arrived in Washington was to sign a commitment to civility, along with almost every other member of my freshman class in the 115th Congress. It was a simple act, yet it was a profound commitment by a new group of over fifty new leaders in our nation's capital. As a member of Congress, I strive to do whatever I can to personally restore faith in our governmental institutions while recognizing the limited role such institutions play. We need to be able to have the confidence that Congress, within its limited scope, can work, that our troops will be provided for, that our home front will be protected, and that equal justice for all will be preserved.

I am a staunch conservative, yet too many of my peers think that we should spend all our time talking about what we are against, failing to cast a vision of what our conservative values and positions can do to move our country forward. Vice President Mike Pence, for years as a congressman and governor, would describe himself as a conservative but one who is "not mad about it." Following my election to Congress, then-governor Pence advised me to be careful in Washington with my retort toward those with whom I disagree. He explained the wisdom of a gentle touch from the microphone on the House floor. He would rise in opposition to another member, beginning his response with words such as, "With all due respect to my colleague from Michigan, who I know loves this country just as much as I do . . ." A response like that can go such a long way.

So many come to politics with righteous indignation that stands in great contrast to the style suggested by Vice President Mike Pence. Some like to think of themselves as being like Christ when he tossed the Temple tables. They are certainly not representing him accurately, though, since he only did that once while being consistently gracious to all. A politician who upends tables regularly will lack the Christ-like or Pence-advised touch needed to convince others. I think, and I believe most citizens would agree, that we should spend more of our time talking about what we are for. We conservatives are for prosperity, security, and freedom. We believe in fighting for what is best for each person and community and not for what simply wins political points. Tabloid political fights and yelling past political opponents can be left behind. Conservative principles and the American people are much too important to play second fiddle to tirades and headline-grabbing charades. The American people deserve serious, thoughtful service from those they entrust to lead. And a change in tone will do so much to attract a new generation to choose public service over other professions.

Civil Society and the Free Market

With the erosion of institutions throughout our society, there are countless opportunities for all of us to do our part. While social scientists continually speak of the self-centeredness and isolation that are increasingly fostered in society, we must recognize that collectively working together helps us hold our society intact. This is the case in government, civil society, communities, churches, Little Leagues, and elsewhere. As a conservative, I believe in the individual, in the right to pursue happiness without a big brother government monitoring every move. Yet I also know that an individual works best when he or she voluntarily works with others.

We can reverse the negative trends we face. One does not have to be a member of Congress to take part. There are plenty of opportunities for all of us to help one another. Society is held together by people in everyday situations providing time and attention to the needs of their communities. It is held together by people who make it a point to be a good mom or dad. It is held together by people who help with the Boy Scouts or join the Rotary Club. It is held together by people who talk with their friends about disagreements and still see a friend and not an enemy.

In addition to civil society, the free market is one of the best examples of what can be gained through interaction, cooperation, and collaboration. When people buy and sell in business, they find ways to get along, work together, and help others. No business can prosper without serving others by providing a product or service that is beneficial to them. And what a beautiful thing, that despite all the political noise on Twitter, businesses seamlessly operate and serve their customers, making America the most materially prosperous nation in history.

There is even working together among businesses to help each other and the community with organizations such as local Chambers of Commerce. Many businesses generously volunteer their money and time to nonprofits serving other needs in the community. Many help train the next generation, while others support local children's and professional sports teams through business sponsorships. So often, the business community sets the example by offering civil, peaceful engagement above the vitriol we see elsewhere. The free market not only makes business partners and friends among people in our communities but does so more broadly, across the world. Trade ensures peace and stability because it allows collaboration.

It is because Washington does not and cannot have all the answers that we need people in real America to be active participants. The contributions of civil society and the free market are critically important. Any role in government should always be performed with the mindset to allow civil society and the free market to flourish. In America we recognize it to be a universal truth that the government exists for the people, not the people for the government. When civil society and the free market have the room they need to improve, society as a whole improves. As the former president of my local Rotary Club, I know firsthand that the center of the universe is not Washington DC but rather Columbia City, Indiana, and communities like it throughout our great country. And that is where we are going to find our next generation of leaders to move our country forward.

The Road Ahead

The way forward will have to be innovative. As times and technologies have changed, civic participation will change too. First, we need to reinvigorate civic participation in our local communicates by re-creating civic organizations. Membership in everything from the Masonic Lodge halls to the local VFW is declining and aging because younger generations are not joining these organizations as they did in years past. We need to re-create the public square, venues for interaction, and opportunities for civil discourse, and our nation's leaders need to lead a conversation about how we do it. It is not productive to debate either ending or curbing social media as an outlet, but it is important that we motivate in-person interactions in our society, especially with our younger generations, to guarantee that they are immersed in civic-minded participation. For me, it was being recruited to join my high school Key Club, a student-led high school membership group chartered by the local Kiwanis Club, of which an uncle and favorite teacher were active members. We need more of that in our schools and in society at large.

Not everyone will want to interact in the same ways and through the same kinds of organizations as before. But we must still find ways that will work. It will be more vital to our future than any law Congress can write. It will look different in New York City than it will in my hometown. It will look different for twenty-five-year-olds than seventy-five-year-olds. But the place to start is not in an anonymous internet post; it is in open dialogue with other people.

Second, we need to raise the importance and relevance of debate again in our society and teach our children and younger generation how to respond without offense. High schools across the nation have seen debate clubs dissipate, but they should consider investing in them at least a fraction as much as they do in athletic clubs. Congress even needs to do its part and elevate the importance of debate, admittedly a disappointing aspect of my new job in the nation's capital. Debate almost always occurs in the middle of the day, while most members are in committees or taking meetings in their offices. Rarely, if ever, does a debate occur on the House floor with a majority of representatives present. The weekly colloquy at the close of the week between current Majority Leader Kevin McCarthy and Minority Whip Steny Hoyer provides perhaps the only true back-and-forth debate from the House floor each week. We must find ways to restore the importance of debate in our culture, presenting both sides of the issues as former generations of Lincolns and Douglasses did in the public square.

When things are political, they need to be addressed openly if we are to find a way to maintain our union of differences. It is promising to see the return of forums such as the debates CNN hosts between Senator Ted Cruz and Senator Bernie Sanders outside of the presidential election cycle. If we can at least talk to each other about our different beliefs, we are already halfway there. The media will have to make some improvements to go beyond just presenting one point of view to a cornered market; it must instead foster the marketplace of ideas. The same goes for the increasingly polarized college campuses, as well as earlier education. The First Amendment is a right that opens doors for a lot of opportunities. Open debate and competition bring with them hope for solutions. But some in the press and education systems seem to think that the answer to harsh disagreement is to curtail discussion altogether.

Finally, we must raise the level of decency in the American political system. I recently toured the Ronald Reagan Library with a veteran and imminently respected member of Congress. When I asked him about his favorite memory of working with President Reagan, he paused and remarked, "I just hope our country can find another leader like him." We need more Reaganesque kindness and optimism in today's conversation.

As a new generation begins to take part in public service, our leaders must rise above the negativity of our current political culture. They must speak up and speak out, but do so with inspiration, humility, and openness to discussion. We need a new set of leaders like Ronald Reagan and John F. Kennedy who will inspire a new generation. We need our current leaders to strive for greater civility if we are to revitalize the call to public service. Such participation must offer the hope of bringing about a greater good if capable young people are to choose it over alternative career paths.

As America was fighting for its independence in 1776, Thomas Paine stated, "These are the times that try men's souls."[17] We, too, face trying times. Thanks to those who have gone before, we have our freedom, but the question remains if we can keep it. It is the task of a new generation who will take up the mantle and answer the call to serve their country in government, the military, and their communities. And it is the task of all citizens to do their part to provide for their families, customers, clients, and friends. America is a nation "of the people, by the people, and for the people." We may lose faith in this or that policy, but we must never give up on the ideal of freedom and justice for all.

Notes

1. J. D. Vance, *Hillbilly Elegy: A Memoir of a Family and Culture in Crisis* (New York: HarperCollins, 2016).

2. Bill Browder, *Red Notice: How I Became Putin's No. 1 Enemy* (London: Bantam Press, 2015).

3. Gordon Wood, *Friends Divided: John Adams and Thomas Jefferson* (New York: Penguin Press, 2017), 279–319.

4. Arthur C. Brooks, "The Thrill of Political Hating," *New York Times*, last modified June 8, 2015, https://www.nytimes.com/2015/06/08/opinion/the-thrill-of-political-hating.html; Arthur C. Brooks, "Empathize with Your Political Foe," *New York Times*, last modified January 21, 2018, https://www.nytimes.com/2018/01/21/opinion/empathize-with-your-political-foe.html.

5. David Streifeld, "'The Internet Is Broken': @ev Is Trying to Salvage It," *New York Times*, last modified May 20, 2017, https://www.nytimes.com/2017/05/20/technology/evan-williams-medium-twitter-internet.html.

6. Sara Salinas, "Facebook Co-Founder Sean Parker Bashes Company, Saying It Was Built to Exploit Human Vulnerability," CNBC, last modified

November 9, 2017, https://www.cnbc.com/2017/11/09/facebooks-sean-parker
-on-social-media.html.

7. James Vincent, "Former Facebook Exec Says Social Media Is Ripping Apart Society," *The Verge*, last modified December 11, 2017, https://www.theverge
.com/2017/12/11/16761016/former-facebook-exec-ripping-apart-society.

8. David A. Moss, *Democracy: A Case Study* (Cambridge MA: Belknap Press of Harvard University Press, 2017), 1–15.

9. Moss, *Democracy: A Case Study.*

10. Robert D. Putnam, *Bowling Alone: The Collapse and Revival of American Community* (New York: Simon & Schuster Paperbacks, 2000).

11. Sebastian Junger, *Tribe: On Homecoming and Belonging* (New York: HarperCollins, 2016).

12. Yuval Levin, *The Fractured Republic: Renewing America's Social Contract in the Age of Individualism* (New York: Basic Books, 2016).

13. John F. Kennedy, *Listening In: The Secret White House Recordings of John F. Kennedy*, ed. Ted Widmer (New York: Hyperion, 2012), 43–50.

14. James Madison, *The Writings of James Madison*, ed. Gaillard Hunt, vol. 3, 1787: *The Journal of the Constitutional Convention* (New York: Knickerbocker Press, 1902), 403.

15. Thomas Spoehr and Bridget Handy, "The Looming National Security Crisis: Young Americans Unable to Serve in the Military," Backgrounder, Heritage Foundation, February 13, 2018, https://www.heritage.org/sites/default
/files/2018–02/bg3282.pdf.

16. Alex Rogers, "Harry Reid: No Regrets over False Romney Charges," *Time*, last modified March 31, 2015, http://time.com/3765158/harry-reid
-mitt-romney-no-taxes/.

17. Thomas Paine, *"Common Sense" and "The American Crisis I"* (New York: Penguin Books, 2012), 189.

8

The Story of Us

Community Cohesion

CHERIE HARDER

Nearly three hundred years ago, when America's Founders staked "their lives, fortunes, and sacred honor" on forming a new nation, they knew it would be a perilous venture. The republic they founded faced invasion from the world's largest empire of the time. The Americans lacked a standing army or navy; the Brits boasted the world's best navy. The colonies composing the new republic were deeply divided on seminal matters of governance, state sovereignty, and slavery and lacked either a history or a talent for cooperation. Taxes were high, embargoes on necessities began, disease was commonplace, and unrest and violence, such as the cruel practice of tarring and feathering, were more widespread and brutal than many history textbooks let on.

The signers of the Declaration of Independence all knew they were gambling their lives and that success was a long shot. Even after their bet paid off and the American Founders escaped the violent end that meets most revolutionaries, they fretted over the future of the new nation. Ben Franklin revealed his own concern as he departed from the Constitutional Convention, where he was queried as to what sort of new government had been established and responded: "A Republic . . . if you can keep it."[1] John Adams noted that "there never was a democracy that did not commit suicide."[2] Fellow Founder James Madison argued in the *Federalist* No. 10 that democracies "have in general been as short in their lives as they have been violent in their deaths."[3]

Their concerns were both historically based and well founded.

Less than a century later, the fledgling republic nearly was lost. Southern states seceded from the Union in defiance of the American creed that all were created equal with inalienable rights. And in preserving the Union, Lincoln renarrated and synthesized the American story as a nation "conceived in liberty, and dedicated to the proposition that all men are created equal."[4]

In the years since the Civil War, the Republic has faced existential challenges—two world wars, seismic divisions over segregation (a division in itself), the Vietnam War, and our current civic alienation and polarization. But a new and toxic contemporary challenge is the growing number of Americans who no longer believe there is a unifying American story with the potential to bridge differences and channel frustration. Gallup recently reported that the percentage of citizens who reported feeling "proud" to be an America fell nearly 20 percentage points between 2003 and a little over a decade later, with the sharpest decline among the young, only a third of whom felt pride in their country.[5]

So who are we? What does it mean to be an American? What is our story?

The idea of "American exceptionalism" has come under attack in recent years, but a nation founded upon a set of ideas is indeed historically exceptional. Nation-states have long been forged along racial, ethnic, religious, and linguistic lines; citizenship for these countries was largely a matter of belonging to a tribe rather than pledging allegiance to a creed. In many countries, nationalism grew out of differentiation among people groups, and power was sought, protected, and transmitted through family patriarchs. The founding of the United States turned this on its head, articulating a set of principles that defined the new country. Historian Gordon Wood, a contributor to this volume, emphasized the momentous rejection of the monarchy and historical norms of inherited political power, stressing that even with the various hypocrisies and shortcomings, as well as the capitulation to the evil of slavery embedded within the Founders' creation, this new form of government truly was revolutionary—an entirely new, if fragile, creation.[6] As Margaret Thatcher once observed, America built its foundation on an idea, but "the European nations are not and can never be like this. They are the product of history and not of philosophy."[7]

That philosophy was broad and sweeping. It included a view of human nature as bent toward self-interest but endowed by God with an intrinsic dignity and worth, with the implication that human selfishness meant that powers should be divided and checked to minimize the possibility for tyranny or abuse (a view later echoed by theologian Reinhold Niebuhr as "man's capacity for justice makes democracy possible; man's capacity for injustice makes democracy necessary").[8] It included a belief in the potential of ordering liberty to maximize freedom and encourage justice and the assertion that each individual, regardless of origin, was endowed by God with "inalienable" rights. The American creed recognized that a free citizenry and a just government could only be achieved by self-government and that self-government required a form of intellectual, moral, and civic formation among citizens. The philosophy also included the declaration that those rights inhered in all humans—that all men and women were created equal—and much of the American story has been the too-slow, injustice-riddled, frequently frustrating unfolding of that vision.

This vision, of course, has not been fully realized, and as a result, the philosophy underpinning it has been criticized as window dressing for the practice of oppression. But it is worth noting that virtually every major American reform movement (abolitionism, woman suffrage, labor reforms, desegregation, etc.) that brought about greater justice and fairness did so in part by appealing to the ideals of America and showing where government policy or societal practice contradicted or fell short of those ideals. As such, reformers sought not only to pass legislation but to persuade their fellow citizens, changing their minds, hearts, and actions, and with them norms and customs, even as they changed the law.

As citizens report feeling more alienated from their government and from each other, it can be easy to forget the vital importance of societal norms and the community involvement and relational bonds that create them.

One of the greatest analysts of the American story was Frenchman Alexis de Tocqueville, who visited America in 1831 intending to study its penal system and provide a recommendation to his home country as to whether the United States offered a worthwhile model to follow. But he was also deeply curious about why the country was flourishing at a time when European nations were not and what lay behind the dynamism of the new nation. Tocqueville headed to Washington DC and was unimpressed. As he traveled more widely, he became convinced that the genius of America was not the legislative process but the "little platoons" of community associations and institutions that largely set societal norms, expectations, and customs. He wrote in *Democracy in America*:

> The customs of the American people are then the peculiar cause which renders that people the only one of the American nations that is able to support a democratic government; and it is the influence of customs that produces . . . prosperity. . . . Too much importance is attributed to legislation, too little to customs. . . . I am convinced that the best possible laws cannot maintain a Constitution in spite of the customs of a country. . . . [I]f I have hitherto failed in making the reader feel the important influence of the practical experience, the habits, the opinions, in short, the customs of the Americans upon the maintenance of institutions, I have failed in the principal object of my work.[9]

Tocqueville would likely argue that the continuance of our story requires maintaining and strengthening the voluntary associations that mediate between the individual and the state, that enable associations and coalitions to work for reform, that help create the norms and customs that sustain the early promise (and correct the injustices) of the American story. But one of the great challenges to the American story is the erosion of the norms and customs that have sustained the American story and the fraying of the relational and community bonds that undergird them.

In his incisive book *The Fractured Republic*, author Yuval Levin argues that since the end of the World War II the American story has followed

a single complex but coherent trajectory . . . of increasing individualism, diversity, dynamism, and liberalization. And it has
come at the cost of dwindling solidarity, cohesion, stability,
authority, and social order. . . . There is an alternative to this
perilous mix of over-centralization and hyper-individualism.
It can be found in the intricate structure of our complex social
topography and in the institutions and relationships that stand
between the isolated individual and the national state. These
begin in loving family attachments. They spread outward to
interpersonal relationships in neighborhoods, schools, workplaces, religious communities, fraternal bodies, civic associations, economic enterprises, activist groups, and the work of
local government. . . . And they conclude in a national identity
that among its foremost attributes is dedicated to the principle
of the equality of the entire human race.[10]

One of the greatest challenges to the American story is the
erosion of the mediating institutions Levin describes. Citizen participation in voluntary groups and associations has
declined precipitously over the last few decades, with the biggest
declines among younger age groups. Time spent with neighbors, in group activities, socializing in person, volunteering,
and sleeping has dwindled; time spent working but also watching, viewing, and surfing the internet has increased. At the
same time, loneliness and feelings of alienation have risen.
Americans are increasingly likely to live alone, to report having few or no close friends, to struggle with feelings of alienation and depression. A survey published by the AARP found
that as many as a third of Americans over the age of forty-five
reported being chronically lonely—up from only one in five a
decade earlier.[11] And other surveys indicate that the loneliest
Americans are the youngest.[12]

If the continuance of the American story depends at least in
part on the connections between citizens and participation in
the broader story, what can be done? Certainly, there are broad
social trends in play, but there are also some simple, concrete
steps that any person can take, including the following:

Teach and learn our story. It is unrealistic to expect citizens to value what they have not been taught and do not understand, and the widespread public ignorance about the basic facts of American history certainly contributes to a devaluing of or indifference to the American story. It is not merely that few Americans can name their senators or any member of the Supreme Court or that a majority of people confuse statements from *The Communist Manifesto* with the Declaration of Independence (although that is indeed the case); more importantly, various studies show an increasing cynicism, coupled with ignorance, about the basics of the American story—why, how, by whom, and for what purposes the United States was created and continues. Few requirements exist to teach civics or social studies to students in elementary and secondary schools. And recent studies show a decline in knowledge of and support for basic First Amendment protections of free speech and religion among college students.

Among the electorate as a whole, the increasing support for authoritarianism, for leaders who will cut through constraints to get things done, suggests a lack of understanding of the American story. It suggests that citizens either don't know or don't value the reasons why the Founders believed it was so vital to limit and check federal powers, why their recognition of individual rights arising from innate dignity was both groundbreaking and essential, and why they stressed self-government as a vital part of the health of the nation.

Teaching the American story necessarily involves exposing its chapters to scrutiny and criticism. But it also enables Americans to develop more informed critiques, to persuade their fellow citizens by reference to shared civic knowledge, and, therefore, to write new future chapters informed by history.

Privilege reading over scanning, surfing, and posting. Decades ago, Marshall McLuhan declared that "the medium is the message," arguing that the mode of communication shapes and biases content—a point sharpened by the advent of social media.[13] Just as it is difficult to discuss philosophy by smoke signal (to borrow an example from Neil Postman), it is also difficult to communicate complex arguments by Facebook or Instagram or the horror and tragedy of violence in video games. McLuhan's warning, "We become what we behold. We shape our tools and then our tools shape us," is particularly salient for those interested in the next chapter of the American story. There is significant evidence that reading, particularly literature, increases not only our empathy, focus, imagination, and capacity for abstract reasoning but also our interest in and commitment to civic engagement. In contrast, time spent consuming electronic media and entertainment is correlated with increased distraction, desensitization, isolation, and aggression. In fact, a recent Census Bureau survey indicated that those who read literature are more likely to be involved in their community, including volunteering, voting, and giving to charity. Whereas 43 percent of literary readers were involved in volunteer or charitable efforts, only 17 percent of nonreaders were.[14] It seems that reading actually helps develop the relational, civic, and intellectual dispositions for self-government, whereas electronic media usage correlates with increased anger, distraction, and alienation.

Join and engage. One of the most important ways to learn, value, and understand the American story is to be part of it through participation in the "little platoons" of civil society. Americans who volunteer and who join churches, synagogues, mosques, community groups, soccer leagues, homeowners associations, school boards, even hobby groups learn the challenges and rewards of both belonging and contributing to community life. Such affiliations force us to learn about our neighbors, to reach across divides, to pursue good things together, to create and observe the rules and processes that guide the pursuit of those goods, and to engage in the act of self-government that underlies the American story and makes the "pursuit of happiness" possible.

Extend hospitality. A potent if modest form of participating in the American story is the simple practice of hospitality. One of the great challenges to civic cohesion has been the dramatic rise of loneliness, with all its attendant pathologies. Loneliness can literally kill its sufferers, causing or exacerbating a range of physical or mental illnesses, including cancer, heart disease, obesity, diabetes, and Alzheimer's. And the havoc wreaked on the body politic is just as sobering. Some of the most difficult and seemingly intractable political problems of our time—growing polarization, a loss of faith in governing institutions, the breakdown of family and community, the decline of civic participation, and the concentration of poverty and addiction in particular rural and urban enclaves—either arise from or are exacerbated by the loss of personal relationships and connections and our growing alienation from each other.

But one of the most effective antidotes to the civic poison of loneliness is hospitality. Merely opening one's home to others also opens possibilities for new or deepening connections and friendships. Whether one extends or receives it, hospitality acts to defuse suspicion, erode barriers to connection, and build up good will—and in doing so, hospitality builds trust, community, and the social bonds necessary for the American story to continue to unfold.

The American story is a checkered one, with much to lament as well as to celebrate, but it includes a historically unprecedented set of ideals and a sustaining promise that allow for the possibility of ever brighter new chapters. Realizing those ideals ultimately depends not only on the machinations of government but on community bonds, associations, norms, and customs that help form citizens and connect them to the American story and to each other. The next American chapter depends on how well we the people (in the words of Ben Franklin) "hang together."

Notes

1. The response, attributed to Benjamin Franklin, occurred at the close of the Constitutional Convention of 1787 and was recorded in the notes of Dr. James McHenry, one of Maryland's delegates to the convention. McHenry's notes were first published in the *American Historical Review* 11 (1906), and the anecdote on page 618 reads: "A lady asked Dr. Franklin Well Doctor what have we got a republic or a monarchy. A republic replied the Doctor if you can keep it." When McHenry's notes were included in *The Records of the Federal Convention of 1787*, ed. Max Farrand, volume 3, appendix A, page 85

(1911, reprinted in 1934), a footnote stated that the date when this anecdote was written is uncertain.

2. John Adams to John Taylor, December 17, 1814, https://founders.archives .gov/documents/Adams/99–02–02–6371.

3. Alexander Hamilton, James Madison, and John Jay, *The Federalist*, ed. Henry Dawson (New York: Charles Scribner, 1863). See https://www .congress.gov/resources/display/content/The+Federalist+Papers#The FederalistPapers-10.

4. Garry Wills, *Lincoln at Gettysburg: The Words That Remade America* (New York: Simon & Schuster, 1992), 263.

5. Jeffrey M. Jones, "New Low of 52% 'Extremely Proud' to Be Americans," Gallup, July 1, 2016, http://news.gallup.com/poll/193379/new-low-extremely -proud-americans.aspx.

6. Gordon Wood, *The Radicalism of the American Revolution* (New York: Vintage Books, 1991).

7. Margaret Thatcher, speech at Hoover Institution Lunch, Four Seasons Hotel, Washington DC, March 8, 1991.

8. Reinhold Niebuhr, *The Children of Light and the Children of Darkness* (New York: Scribner's, 1944), ix.

9. Alexis de Tocqueville, *Democracy in America,* ed. and trans. Harvey Mansfield and Delba Winthrop (Chicago: University of Chicago Press, 2000).

10. Yuval Levin, *The Fractured Republic: Renewing America's Social Contract in the Age of Individualism* (New York: Basic Books, 2017).

11. G. Oscar Anderson, "Loneliness among Older Adults: A National Survey of Adults 45+," AARP, September 2010, https://www.aarp.org/research /topics/life/info-2014/loneliness_2010.html.

12. Katrina Trinko, "Gen Z Is the Loneliest Generation, and It's Not Just Because of Social Media," *USA Today*, May 3, 2018, https://www.usatoday .com/story/opinion/2018/05/03/gen-z-loneliest-generation-social-media -personal-interactions-column/574701002.

13. Marshall McLuhan, *Understanding Media: The Extensions of Man* (New York: Mentor, 1964).

14. "To Read or Not to Read," Research Report #47, November 2007, National Endowment for the Arts, https://www.arts.gov/sites/default/files/ToRead.pdf.

9

An American Community

NIKOLAS GVOSDEV

Twenty-five years ago, sociologist and public intellectual Amitai Etzioni expressed his concerns about polling data that defined the United States not as a political community but as a place where one could do as one pleased—the ultimate refuge for individualism. He was echoed in his worries by Mary Ann Glendon, the Learned Hand Professor of Law at Harvard Law School who uttered the memorable phrase that, taken to its logical conclusion, such a view would mean that "we roam at large in a land of strangers."[1] Etzioni's 1994 work, *The Spirit of Community*, written amid the surge of intercommunal violence that, after the end of the Cold War, engulfed a number of formerly peaceful multiethnic and diverse societies, was an effort to reconceptualize American national identity in a way that would engender, as he put it, "a shared vision and commitment that all share a common fate."[2] This statement in turn was built on the observation famously crafted by Benedict Anderson in *Imagined Communities*, that any successful nation that hoped to endure would have to engender in its citizens the belief that "in the minds of each lives the image of their communion," even if they don't know each other personally.[3] For Etzioni and the other communitarians, participation in the American body politic could not simply be equated to a random agglomeration of people who happened to share geographic proximity or economic relationships; that participation must include an acceptance and internalization of the sense of belonging to a community from which rights flowed and to which responsibilities were owed.

Etzioni's book and the formal launch of the communitarian movement was met, in some quarters, with respectful criticism that suggested that his and others' concerns about the strength of American identity were overly pessimistic. Some of the responses relied on the reading of "American exceptionalism" as defined by Ian Tyrrell: "a belief that the U.S. follows a path of history different from the laws or norms that govern other countries."[4] They argued that the United States had successfully found the formula to reconciling its ethnic, geographic, and religious diversity as summed up under the motto *e pluribus unum* in a way that could also enhance the deepening of its democratic form of governance and an expansion of rights and privileges. The economic boom of the 1990s and the immediate post-9/11 environment both supported this notion of the strength and resilience of American identity—that common pursuit of the "American Dream" on "American soil" would mitigate Glendon's concern about roaming in a land of strangers. The events of the last several years, however, have demonstrated, the tenets of American exceptionalism notwithstanding, that the United States is subject to the same political and sociological trends that impact and shape other nations. This process has been aided by technological change that enables individuals to disassociate from their geographically proximate neighbors in favor of forging stronger and closer bonds via the internet. It has also been aided by the ease of long-distance travel to meet like-minded individuals who share similar ethnic, linguistic, or philosophical backgrounds and by the phenomenon of the "big sort," whereby a search for subgroup affinities drives choices about where to live. A crucial factor in the success of the "melting pot" in earlier generations—the one-way nature of the trip to the United States and the difficulties in overcoming the tyranny of distance—no longer applies.[5] Moreover, the United States is not immune from the possibility of intercommunal strife or the possibility that its sense of national unity could be ruptured. What is striking, in the aftermath of the 2016 presidential elections, is the degree of narrative collapse—the loss of faith in both the existence and the unifying power of the American Dream, uncertainties over the role the United States ought to be playing the world, and even whether there exists a commonly shared narrative about what defines "Americanness" that can serve as the basis for a shared civic and political identity. The heated debate in 2018 over the nature and purpose of the census further illustrates growing divides over what constitutes membership in the American nation.

At this moment when there are discussions on how to rejuvenate or create anew a sense of shared American identity, it might be useful to consider how other multiethnic and diverse societies are managing the question of *e pluribus unum* in the twenty-first century. Two countries in particular may have relevance: the Russian Federation, which, like the United States, is a continent-spanning nation; and Switzerland, a multilingual federal republic.

After the collapse of the Soviet Union, the newly emerged Russian Federation found itself without any clear foundation for national identity. The USSR had been predicated on an ideological union of socialist states working together to achieve a new society in which the proletariat had no nationality and old markers such as nationality and religious affiliation would fade away in a process known as *sliianiye* (merging), producing a new *Sovietskii narod* (Soviet people), a Communist version of the melting pot. The rejection of Marxism-Leninism as the ideological foundation of the state, however, meant that post-Soviet Russia needed to find another basis for common citizenship and political life.

Like the Soviet Union, the Russian Federation is a patchwork of different national, ethnic, linguistic, and religious groups. As the USSR was dissolving, one option would have been to continue the process of ethnic self-determination, by which nonethnically Russian components would gain independence and separate status, while ethnically Russian areas belonging to other Soviet republics would join with parts of the Russian Federation to form a Russian ethnostate. There were a number of problems, however, with this approach. Many of the regions designated as nonethnically Russian republics either did not have a plurality of the titular nationality living there or were already tightly integrated with surrounding regions. The collapse of the USSR also left up to twenty-five million people claiming affiliation as ethnic Russians outside the borders of the federation, and the creation of an ethnic Russian ethnostate would open a Pandora's box of instability.[6]

Sergei Stankevich, one of Boris Yeltsin's advisors, wrote an essay, "Russia in Search of Itself," in which the question of finding a durable national identity for the post-Soviet Russian Federation was placed as one of the most critical tasks of the new administration.[7] He hoped that a new sense of national identity would come about based not on ethnicity but on the belief that "Russians" were people united by a common task, taking part in a shared endeavor, with the emphasis being on belonging to a shared state. In the first years after the Soviet collapse, there was an effort to cultivate a so-called civic nationalism that would avoid "blood and soil" definitions. In particular, the new government stressed a definition of "Russian" as epitomized by the term *rossiiane*, a nonethnic term indicating someone who is a citizen of the Russian state, as opposed to *russkii*, an ethnic Russian. As part of the effort to encourage the cultivation of a nonethnic sense of nationality, the Yeltsin administration ordered the removal of any designation of ethnicity from official passports and documents.

This effort faltered because the core elements of a new civic Russianness lacked depth and did not resonate with the general public. Starting in the second half of the Yeltsin administration and continuing during the Vladimir Putin years, the Russian government has focused instead on balancing the dominance of the Russian ethnic core with recognizing and accommodating the country's ethnic, religious, and cultural pluralism. It has done so by utilizing a strategy that I and others have described as "managed pluralism."[8] Ethnic Russian identity and the Orthodox Christian religion are the predominant elements that define Russianness, with a recognition that other groups and elements have been grafted onto, joined with, or allied with this core. "Managed pluralism" sets the boundary lines for the acceptable degrees of divergence from the preferred norm. Thus, in the religious sphere, even recognizing differences in theology and practice, a stress in contemporary Russian discourse is to highlight common Russian or Eurasian features that distinguish Russia's Buddhists, Muslims, Jews, and Orthodox Christians and differentiate them from their coreligionists in Europe, the Middle East, and East Asia, providing a basis for shared values.

The stage managing of the official memorial ceremonies on the Day of Russian Unity is indicative of the managed pluralism approach at work. At the wreath-laying ceremony that takes place at the Monument to Minin and Pozharsky in Red Square in Moscow, the Russian president is accompanied by the patriarch of the Russian Orthodox Church, after which the president brings forward the heads of the Jewish, Muslim, Buddhist, Old Believer, Roman Catholic, and Evangelical Baptist communities. It is a visually impressive display of Russia's diversity, but it also highlights that the ethnic Russian and religious Russian Orthodox identity holds the primacy of honor and position.[9]

The Russian system is buttressed by two additional factors. The first is that there exists a clear and defined pathway for non-Russians to be defined as "ethnic Russians," steps that have been taken over the years by a number of individuals from non-Russian ethnicities, notably Jews, to become assimilated into the Russian core if they so choose. The second is that there is an understanding throughout society that whenever there are competing claims to be adjudicated between different ethnic and religious groups in society, primacy is given to the ethnic Russian and religious Russian Orthodox narrative as setting the norm. This is especially true when historical events are being assessed. The "gathering of the land," which defined the transformation of the small city-state principality of Moscow into a Eurasian realm spanning eleven time zones, is viewed as positive, and while those individuals who resisted this process might be valorized for individual courage or determination, the act itself must be condemned. The closing epilogue to the 2012 film *The Horde*, which depicts relations during the Middle Ages between Russians and Tatars, is a paean to the role of the Russian state in gathering together the different pieces of the central Eurasian plain into a single entity, grafting non-Russian peoples and cultures onto an ethnic Russian core—a theme also reflected in the national anthem's celebration of "fraternal peoples in eternal union."

President Putin, in addressing Western experts attending the Valdai Discussion Club in 2004, praised the Russian experience in fostering a common sense of nationhood amid the cultural, religious, and linguistic diversity of the Eurasian steppes. The Russian approach, to some extent, reflects what was the traditional American experience as well in forging a national identity, which is why some American thinkers, especially on the paleoconservative side, have spoken approvingly of the Russian experiment as relevant to the United States. They hark back to sentiments such as those expressed by John Adams. In presenting his credentials to King George III of Great Britain on June 1, 1785, Adams defined the new American nation as being ethnically, culturally, and religiously connected to England, arguing that the two nations were linked by "the same language, a similar religion, and kindred blood."[10] Adams was certainly aware, even disregarding the American population of African descent, both enslaved and free, as well as the Native Americans, that the newly independent state contained immigrants and settlers from other parts of Europe (Irish, Dutch, French Huguenots, and Swedes, for instance), but he expected that these other groups would intermarry and assimilate into an English American norm.

Building on that observation, Samuel Huntington has argued (notably in his 2004 treaties *Who Are We?*) that U.S. national identity rests on Anglo-Saxon and Protestant foundations as shaped by experiences in the New World, but that identity is also characterized by an inclusive attitude that allows others a pathway to assimilate into it.[11] To some extent, U.S. identity remains defined by some of these parameters—the retention of English as the language of the public square, for instance, and the permeation of the Protestant experience (its approach to social ethics and its congregational models) into how Americans of all backgrounds conceive of their religious life and how civil society ought to be organized. Indeed, the work done by R. Stephen Warner and Judith G. Wittner on the religious experiences of new immigrants in the United States shows how the American Protestant ethos infuses not only non-Protestant but even non-Christian communities in the United States, although Etzioni and others dispute how "Protestant" some of those features are, arguing that they were already present in those traditions.[12]

Yet there are major roadblocks to reframing contemporary U.S. national identity along such lines. First, it must be noted that the Russian effort to manage pluralism requires a much higher degree of government imposition to even have a chance at success; such an imposition would certainly run into numerous constitutional challenges in the U.S. context. Moreover, despite Russia's incredible ethnic, religious, and linguistic diversity, more than 80 percent of Russian citizens self-identify as ethnic Russians, and some 74 percent claim affiliation to one very specific Christian tradition: Orthodoxy. A similar percentage of Americans may describe themselves as Christian, but in the U.S. experience, hundreds of competing and clashing denominations prevent any one tradition from exercising primacy, and the attempts in the late nineteenth century to present the Episcopal Church as the de facto "American national" church—as evidenced in the 1893 congressional charter for the creation of a "national cathedral" in Washington—would not be accepted today. And despite Adams's paeans to "kindred blood," Anglo-Saxons are a minority, outnumbered by those claiming descent from Celts, Germans, Latins (of both the Old and New World varieties), and Slavs. Europe's share in the overall American demographic is slipping vis-à-vis other parts of the world. Bowing to this reality, in 2018 Harvard, America's oldest university, removed from its alma mater a reference to the "stock of the Puritans" because an absolute majority of Harvard students now claim no such descent or identity.

The Russian Federation model would also not be acceptable to many segments of American society that oppose any effort to designate as the norm a particular "model" of Americanness based on specific ethnic and religious criteria, thus creating a multitiered system in which certain ethnicities and traditions are privileged as more American than others. Instead of looking for a core identity, it might be better to reimagine America as a mosaic of different pieces that coexist in a single political and economic community. If, as journalist Bill Bishop has argued, the United States is currently undergoing a "big sort," in which groups of like-minded Americans separate into distinct geographic communities, then finding a different approach to fostering unity might be more appropriate than adopting a one-size-fits-all identity.[13]

In the 1959 edition of *Out of Our Past: The Forces That Shaped Modern America*, Carl Degler coined a new way of envisioning American identity: "The metaphor of the melting pot is unfortunate and misleading. A more accurate analogy would be a salad bowl, for, although the salad is an entity, the lettuce can still be distinguished from the chicory, the tomatoes from the cabbage."[14] The principal objection to the "salad bowl" metaphor is that there is no basis for a common identity and thus, over time, the cohesiveness of the society will erode. Yet for defenders of the salad bowl approach, the experience of the Swiss Union, which holds together as a strong state with a cohesive and powerful sense of common identity despite being comprised of several distinct national groups, seems to hold lessons for a more diverse United States. In particular, Switzerland seems to disprove the contention of the English Only movement that imposition of a common language is necessary for both national unity and the preservation of republican governance.

In the Middle Ages, cantons in the valleys of the Swiss Alps began to band together to resist the depredations of the larger empires and great powers that surrounded them. In the nineteenth century, during the efforts to create united nation-states that led to the emergence of modern France, Italy, and Germany, the French, German, and Italian portions of Switzerland eschewed union with their coethnics in favor of retaining their confederation. At the same time, efforts to try and create a Swiss identity (along the lines of the Russian model, using the German Swiss as the core definer of "Swissness") was resisted. Instead, a "Swiss" identity is invested in the federation and how the unity of the federation has enabled the cantons and communes to resist losing their autonomy and being incorporated into larger European entities. The Swiss tend to describe their union using the German term *Eidgenossenschaft*, usually translated as "confederation" but drawing on an older meaning of a fellowship based on mutually binding promises, in this case, the oaths for mutual defense and assistance that bind together German, French, Italian, and Romansch cantons and Protestant and Catholic religions. These documents frame a common narrative that helps to generate a uniquely Swiss identity. A lack of linguistic and religious unity is also counterbalanced by a sense of geographic particularism that is framed by the Alps and their valleys, which helped to cement the notion of Switzerland as a distinct entity. Moreover, the realities of life as they evolved in the Alps meant that, despite cultural pluralism, there were common practices and lifestyles that helped to define a common identity.[15]

The modern Swiss Union is a decentralized federation. One becomes Swiss by being a part of a canton or commune—and it is that sovereign unit, not the federation, that confers status. One conforms to the norms and values—and, most importantly, language—of the canton. A Swiss citizen who moves to a different canton or commune might be a resident of that locality, but his or her citizenship will still be connected to his or her place of origin. He or she will be "Swiss," as opposed to being a foreigner, but will still be viewed as a "guest" in another canton. Moreover, someone moving from Zurich to Geneva or to Ticino cannot insist on obtaining services in German, for instance, or insist that the practices and norms—and, more importantly, rights and privileges—enjoyed in Zurich must equally apply in other cantons. For matters that are reserved to the federation, Swiss law prevails, but on most issues, local preferences carry greater weight. For instance, there is no state church in Switzerland, but cantons can give official status to the Roman Catholic or Swiss Reformed Church. Swiss identity thus rests on the three levels of municipality, canton, and federation.[16]

Extending Degler's metaphor, Switzerland is the "bowl" in which the salad ingredients of the commonwealth are sheltered—but the salad ingredients are free to remain apart and separate and do not need to mingle. Survey data indicate that in terms of work and permanent residence, significant numbers of Swiss do not cross the linguistic dividing lines within the country, most notably, the Röstigraben, which separates the German and French zones. Many Swiss do not cross between the French and German areas and the Italian and Romansch regions. Ironically, despite a 2004 federal directive that Swiss children must learn not only the language of their canton but also at least one other Swiss language, there is now a push in Switzerland to have English—a language with no historical roots in the country—be taught as the uniform second language across the country so that French, German, Italian, and Romansch speakers would all have a single guaranteed intercommunal language.[17]

At an earlier point in its history, the Swiss experience was more relevant to the United States, particularly when most Americans identified much more strongly with their specific state than with the country as a whole—reflected in the usage during the first decades after 1776 of the term "United States" as a plural rather than a singular entity. But this approach was eroded by the high degree of mobility and movement within the country, aided and abetted by the constitutional provision (Article IV, section 2) that "the Citizens of each State shall be entitled to all Privileges and Immunities of Citizens in the several States." A New Yorker moving to Texas, after establishing residency, did not have to undergo a separate naturalization process to acquire the rights of citizenship in his or her new home. Moreover, as new states entered the Union, even if they were initially French, Spanish, or even Hawaiian speaking (Louisiana or California or Hawaii), no provision was made to enshrine those languages as official, meaning that newcomers could be required to learn those languages in order to become citizens of those states.[18]

The Swiss model is also less relevant to the U.S. experience because diversity in the United States, unlike in Switzerland, is not juridically tied to specific geographic regions. There are significant communities of Spanish or Chinese speakers located far from the American Southwest or Pacific Coast. Moreover, a key element in the forging of a Swiss identity—the threat of outside conquest—has been far less relevant for the United States, which enjoys the luxury of the moat provided by the Pacific and Atlantic and the land borders with Canada and Mexico, neither of which has ever posed an existential threat to the United States. The Swiss salad bowl came into existence precisely because in the absence of a Swiss Union, cantons feared being absorbed into a greater France, Germany, or Italy. While the threat posed first by the French Empire and then by the British forced the original thirteen colonies to band together rather than go their separate ways, the American Union, at least for the last 150 years, has been couched in positive terms (affinities shared among the population) rather than in negative ones (resistance to outside pressure). Finally, any attempts to move the United States closer to the Swiss model would run up against the constitutional roadblock of the Fourteenth Amendment, the Equal Protection Clause, which would preclude the extensive autonomy that Swiss cantons have to set many of their policies with regard to language, citizenship, and social policies. For instance, the ruling that the Fourteenth Amendment makes the Bill of Rights binding on state governments precludes New York or Alabama from establishing specific religious denominations at the state level—a provision that is lacking in the Swiss constitutional order. The amendment also prevents Georgia from having standards for naturalizing immigrants different from those in Oregon.

• • •

The Russian model of managed pluralism, based on a defined ethnic and cultural yardstick supplied by the majority (Orthodox Russians), does not provide a workable template for developing a new sense of American identity based on identifying an ethnic core that defines Americanness. The Swiss model of multiculturalism and devolved federalism works because there are sufficient countervailing tendencies to hold the union together—features that are, however, lacking in the American context. Moreover, the unhappy experience of Lebanon or Cyprus shows what happens when subnational communal affiliations are allowed to override national identity as the primary claimant on a person's loyalty.

Yet even if the Russian or Swiss model is not applicable in

toto, elements from their experience should be part of any conversation about renewing a sense of American national identity. A diverse country needs to have markers for a common identity and some elements of a shared narrative that help to define the reasons for the community's existence and why it is worth defending and preserving. These observations also coincide with the communitarian perspective, which stresses the importance of sharing values in a common identity to create strong, resilient communities capable of engendering loyalty—but also to allow a high degree of freedom for individuals and communities to form subcommunities within the larger framework. As Etzioni expressed in 2011, a "good citizen" should willingly undertake a series of basic responsibilities for the common good of the nation, but the nation, in return, should allow him or her the freedom to follow his or her own preferences wherever possible.[19]

Thus, Etzioni and other communitarians reject an assimilationist model that posits the existence of an ideal type of "real American," but they also recognize the dangers to unity and cohesion that unbounded multiculturalism can pose. The challenge is to find a set of shared values that can foster identification with and loyalty to a single national community and to one's fellow citizens without requiring all types of particularity and differentiation to be abandoned. Here, America's traditional commitment both to federalism—that despite protection of a series of rights common to all Americans, the country can accept a degree of divergence and particularism from state to state—and to freedom of association—allowing people the right to gather in specific ethnic, religious, cultural, linguistic, political, and philosophical communities—provides a balance between unity and diversity.

In 2011 Etzioni launched the Diversity within Unity platform, summing up the communitarian approach. As the founding document notes, the platform

> presumes that all members of a given society will fully respect and adhere to those basic values and institutions that are considered part of the basic shared framework of the society. At the same time, every group in society is free to maintain its distinct

subculture—those policies, habits, and institutions that do not conflict with the shared core—and a strong measure of loyalty to its country of origin, as long as this does not trump loyalty to the society in which it lives if these loyalties come into conflict. Respect for the whole and respect for all is at the essence of our position.[20]

What does this mean in the American context? For starters, it posits that the starting basis of American identity is found in the commitment that Americans make to support democratic political institutions, to embrace legal concepts of the Constitution and the Bill of Rights, and to practice social and religious tolerance—none of which require any specific ethnic, religious, or linguistic background. In other words, this sense of Americanness is a result not of blood affiliation but of commitment to a set of principles. This is the core of the American *Eidgenossenschaft*—the oaths we take to each other as Americans.

One could argue that these commitments could extend across the globe and that there is nothing, other than the reference to specific constitutional documents, particularly American about it. However, these commitments take place within the context of the specific set of territories where this experiment in republican governance occurs—North America—amid the social, political, and economic institutions that create the "salad bowl" in which the American nation is contained and defined. As the communitarians have observed, any viable or successful community is exclusive in nature. It must have the ability to define its limits and its memberships; otherwise, it cannot retain its cohesion. This "bowl" has been constructed by the generations of those who have lived within it and augmented by the arrival of newcomers who also join in this common task. As Etzioni himself has noted, "As Americans, we are aware of our different origins but also united by a joint future and fate."[21]

The United States, which so consciously patterned many of its institutions on Roman ones, is also in a position to emulate the concept of Romanitas as first expressed by the lawyer Tertullian in the third century. Romanitas (literally, Romanness) could be undertaken by anyone living within the empire by accepting Roman law and political values, by using Latin as their lingua franca, and by taking part in the political life of the Roman state without having to give up local or particular affiliations, including in religion and language.[22] By the time that all free-born males were granted citizenship by the Edict of Caracalla in 211, Romanitas was no longer identified with ethnic descent from the original residents of the city of Rome, yet it remained a cohesive identity that could still distinguish Romans from non-Romans.[23] This template is remarkably adaptable to the American experience.

American identity must also rest on a shared set of narratives and heroes. If a country bases its identity in part on idealistic aspirations, then it must confront the reality that flawed human beings often fall short of those standards. Rather than delegitimizing the titans of prior generations, a renewed sense of American nationhood would respect their achievements while acknowledging their failings. This can be done in part by embracing an evolutionary approach to American identity, that it has not emerged full-grown but has evolved from an original germinal state into more complex and richer forms. The Puritans and Pilgrims who wanted to create a city on a hill in the New World both committed violence against the existing native populations and had a very circumscribed definition of who should be permitted in that city, but the vision they followed is one we still embrace and celebrate, even if we now reject some of their specific propositions. That the United States in 1789 allowed slavery and denied the franchise to women should not negate the fact that America was, for its time, the freest country in the world. The Constitution was created to allow (largely) peaceful evolution in order to expand the scope of rights and those entitled to citizenship—in other words, to expand membership in the national community beyond blood and descent.

Etzioni reminds us that "nobody can bond with seven billion people, and almost everyone feels more responsibility toward those closest to them."[24] Shared participation in and celebration of the unfinished and ongoing American experiment is the best way to create and cement the bonds of fellowship and citizenship among Americans.

Notes

1. Mary Ann Glendon, *Rights Talk: The Impoverishment of Political Discourse* (New York: Free Press, 1991), 77.

2. Amitai Etzioni, *The Spirit of Community* (New York: Simon and Schuster, 1994), 54.

3. Benedict Anderson, *Imagined Communities: Reflections on the Origins and Spread of Nationalism* (London: Verso, 2006), 6.

4. Ian Tyrrell, "What, Exactly, Is 'American Exceptionalism'?," *The Week*, October 21, 2016, http://theweek.com/articles/654508/what-exactly-american-exceptionalism.

5. These were factors that in turn helped drive the types of assimilation described in Milton M. Gordon, *Assimilation in American Life: The Role of Race, Religion and National Origins* (New York: Oxford University Press, 1964).

6. For a good overview of the attempts to forge post-Soviet Russian national identity, see Yuri Teper, "Official Russian Identity Discourse in Light of the Annexation of Crimea: National or Imperial?," *Post-Soviet Affairs* 32, no. 4 (2016): 378–96.

7. Sergei Stankevich, "Russia in Search of Itself," *National Interest* 28 (Summer 1992): 47–51.

8. See, for instance, Nikolas K. Gvosdev, "Managed Pluralism and Civil Religion in Post-Soviet Russia," in *Civil Society and the Search for Justice in Russia*, ed. Christopher Marsh and Nikolas K. Gvosdev (Lanham MD: Lexington, 2002), 75–88.

9. Footage of the 2017 Day of National Unity can be viewed at https://www.youtube.com/watch?v=gqyjzusCjf4.

10. As related in a letter from John Adams to John Jay, June 2, 1785, and archived at https://founders.archives.gov/documents/Adams/06–17–02–0078.

11. Samuel Huntington, *Who Are We? The Challenges to American National Identity* (New York: Simon and Schuster, 2004).

12. See, for instance, R. Stephen Warner and Judith G. Wittner, eds., *Gatherings in Diaspora: Religious Communities and the New Immigration* (Philadelphia PA: Temple University Press, 1998).

13. Bill Bishop with Robert G. Cushing, *The Big Sort: Why the Clustering of Like-Minded Americans Is Tearing Us Apart* (Boston: Houghton Mifflin Co., 2008).

14. Carl N. Degler, *Out of Our Past: The Forces That Shaped Modern America* (New York: Harper Perennial, 1959, 1970, 1984), 296.

15. This section on Switzerland draws on Wolf Linder, *Swiss Democracy: Possible Solutions to Conflicts in Multicultural Societies*, 3rd ed. (Houndmills, Basingstoke: Palgrave Macmillan, 2010).

16. For more on this, see, for instance, Marc Helbling, "Switzerland: Contentious Citizenship Attribution in a Federal State," *Journal of Ethnic and Migration Studies* 36, no. 5 (2010): 793–809.

17. "Italian 'Ignored' by Swiss Schools in Language Wars," *The Local*, July 11, 2016, https://www.thelocal.ch/20160711/italian-ignored-by-swiss-schools -in-language-wars.

18. These points are discussed in Peter H. Schuck, "Citizenship in Federal Systems," *American Journal of Comparative Law* 48, no. 2 (April 2000): 195–226.

19. Amitai Etzioni, "Citizenship in a Communitarian Perspective," *Ethnicities* 11, no. 3 (2011): 336.

20. The platform is archived at the Communitarian Network site, https:// communitariannetwork.org/diversity-within-unity.

21. Quoted in Shannon Latkin Anderson, *Immigration, Assimilation, and the Cultural Construction of American National Identity* (New York: Routledge, 2016), 200.

22. See the discussion in David E. Wilhite, *Ancient African Christianity: An Introduction to a Unique Context and Tradition* (London: Routledge, 2017), 65–66.

23. Michael Dewar, "Multi-ethnic Armies in Virgil, Lucan, and Claudian: Intertextuality, War, and the Ideology of Romanitas," *Syllecta Classica* 14 (2003): 143–59.

24. Amitai Etzioni, "We Must Not Be Enemies," *American Scholar*, December 5, 2016, https://theamericanscholar.org/we-must-not-be-enemies/#.

10

A Dream for Anyone and Everyone

MARKOS MOULITSAS

I t's easy to craft a single, unifying American narrative when that story is told by a single group of people. A one-sided story can ignore minority voices, dissident viewpoints, and inconvenient or embarrassing facts, which is why the story the dominant Anglo white majority crafted—written by and for themselves—was never quite an accurate reflection of America's real history.

Theirs wasn't a narrative about slaves, dragged a hemisphere away, sold and traded like cattle. Indeed, an entire political party—until recently holding all levels of power—continues to fight to honor the generals and politicians who fought to preserve that system.

Their narrative was never about North America's Native tribes, their people wiped out in savage genocide, their land stripped away by a hungry, expansionist America.

It wasn't about the Chinese brought in to build railroads, or Japanese interned in concentration camps, or Latinos doing the crap work hidden from public view, or an ingrained culture of sanctioned bigotry and discrimination that is championed and perpetuated to this very day, from corporate boardrooms to the ballot box.

That story wasn't about the poor. And it certainly wasn't about women, all but invisible in the history books.

Those people weren't part of the story, even though America could not have been built without them, because they didn't feed the ego-driven narrative that white men created and "tamed" the greatest country on Earth. And when media was dominated by only a handful of media outlets, it was easy to control the flow of information. TV, radio, and newspapers promoted the story of the "American Dream," one of upward mobility and rising standards of living and homeownership, replete with pictures of smiling white suburban families, all the while ignoring the American underclass, denied even a *chance* at that dream. It was easy to live a lie when dissonant chords were muted in the mainstream.

The internet and social media revolutions dramatically changed that equation, with infinite media outlets reflecting every possible group, whether demographic, ideological, cultural, or otherwise. The traditional gatekeepers collapsed, bringing a whole new world of experiences and realities to the forefront. And all those once-invisible groups, long relegated to background noise, got a chance to step up. And boy, did they ever!

Their stories have laid bare the *real* America, one that can be grim, ugly, and depressing. How could one talk proudly of the "American Dream" when black men are being indiscriminately murdered by police across America? How could one be proud of our democracy when Republicans' first order of business, when given the chance to govern, has been to limit access to the ballot box for communities of color and young people?

How could we take pride in our political system when the presidential candidate receiving the *least* amount of votes was elected president not just once but *twice* in twenty years? How can we look at our fellow Americans with affection when so many voted for an overt misogynistic bigot and racist, surrounded by anti-Semites and white supremacists? How can we even take an entire political party—the Republicans—seriously when they have surrendered themselves to Russia in a naked quest for power?

How can we speak of love and acceptance when too many people would deny loving same-sex couples the rights and benefits of matrimony? How can we even talk about *being* American when conservatives consider people like me (an immigrant from El Salvador, from two immigrant parents) to be illegitimate? How can we talk about equality when women have been systematically subjected to harassment and assault by powerful men, shamed and coerced into silence? How can we claim to have learned from history when the president and his followers have taken anti-Semitism out of the shadows and back to the public forefront, leaving assaults, vandalism, and bloody synagogues in their wake?

In this fragmented multimedia landscape, surfacing long-dormant and suppressed voices, we began to glimpse the real America, one that didn't quite fit the rosy narrative long propagated by the white male–dominated majority. Yet rather than embrace these stories in the quest for a more equitable, just, and fair America, conservative white men—the beneficiaries of America's fake history—have lashed out in fury, angered by their perceived loss of power.

Indeed, that emerging reality has been so difficult to process, so hard to take, that American conservatives *literally* built an alternate reality bubble to protect themselves against it. They conquered talk radio, supported a cadre of best-selling conservative authors, built an entire cable network to twist the news to their advantage. And when they had all the conservative media they needed, they kept building more outlets anyway, like Breitbart.

If the American narrative could no longer be whitewashed, why, conservatives would create their *new* whitewashed version of it, one in which racism didn't exist, the LGBTQ community undermined good Christian values, virtuous women obeyed their men faithfully, and our country, blessed by our Creator, could do no wrong. It was an expensive and sophisticated way to stick their fingers in their ears and scream "nyah nyah nyah nyah I CAN'T HEAR YOU" at the top of their lungs.

And since no media bubble is airtight, conservatives decided to label anything that slipped through as "fake news," egged on by their president himself. Objective truth no longer mattered, easily countered with "alternative facts," as Trump advisor Kellyanne Conway famously claimed while defending one of Trump's endless lies. What better way to shrug off unwelcome or unhelpful news and information that filters down to their ears than to simply wave it off as untrue? So what if photographic evidence clearly shows paltry attendance at that inauguration? "Alternative facts" proved otherwise!

Even those things that once united us have lost their power. You have conservatives, led by popular-vote loser Donald Trump, attacking American football because some players have the temerity to *kneel* in protest of police brutality in their communities. Fox News' executive vice president, John Moody, attacked the U.S. Olympic Committee for touting an "embarrassing laundry list of how many African-Americans, Asians and openly gay athletes" represented our nation at the 2018 Winter Olympics. The biggest international sporting success story for the United States has been the women's national soccer team, but given they are a combination of soccer, a *foreign* sport, and *strong women,* their international dominance has had limited mass appeal. The Oscars are now an annual battle pitting conservatives against a Hollywood they see arrayed against them.

Therefore, how can we, as Americans, talk about a unified American story when we *can't even agree on basic facts and reality* and when a huge chunk of America is actively practicing the politics of exclusion? How can we craft a unified American narrative when the older white men who dominate the economic, media, and political spheres refuse to include young, female, brown, nonstraight, and non-Christian voices in that story?

Trump residential advisor and overall Svengali Steve Bannon warned that "women are going to take charge of society." This was bad, supposedly, because this "anti-patriarchy movement would end 10,000 years of recorded history. This is coming. This is real."[1] Vice President Mike Pence claims that gay couples signaled "societal collapse" and that it wasn't discrimination to prevent same-sex marriage; instead, it was enforcement of "God's idea."[2] Trump's White House bizarrely refused to mention the six million Jews murdered by Nazis on his first Holocaust Remembrance Day while in office, claiming that their omission made the statement more "inclusive" because the Romani, gays, and the disabled were also murdered in concentration camps.[3] As shocking as that was, it wasn't surprising, given Trump was being advised by Sebastian Gorka, an out-and-out anti-Semite. And Trump himself can't help his steady stream of racist behavior, from refusing to aggressively condemn Nazis and the KKK marching in Charlottesville in support of Confederate statues; to calling Haiti, my own El Salvador, and African nations "shithole countries" (while praising lily-white Norway); to his first and original classic: equating Mexican immigrants to rapists.[4] At least he's honest about his bigotry, proudly declaring himself a "nationalist," fully understanding the word's racist heritage.

Thus, those right-wing racist, sexist, bigoted, homophobic, and xenophobic voices aren't fringe, they are literally the people running this country. And even if Republicans get swept out eventually by a coalition of America's rising electorate (African Americans, Asians, Latinos, young voters, single women, and white allies), we cannot have a unifying American narrative as long as a movement dedicated to perpetuating those "isms" continues to draw significant support.

A truly unified American story must first start with equality. That truth is so self-evident that Thomas Jefferson led with it in his Declaration of Independence. "All men are created equal." So you can't have Republicans championing policies that restrict voting rights, that lock in unequal school funding mechanisms, that permit unequal policing and a racially biased justice system, that encourage unequal pay in workplaces, or that treat any demographic group or people as less legitimate and deserving than any other. Talking about equality is both true to the roots of our nation and relevant to our multicultural future.

Our national story also speaks of tolerance and acceptance. In a country of such diversity—demographic, cultural, and ideological—we have to be willing to comfortably live alongside people who might look, talk, eat, think, and sound different from us. Unity does not mean uniformity. It means that all of us, regardless of our backgrounds, are working toward a common purpose, and America has always practiced this kind of radical acceptance:

> Give me your tired, your poor,
> Your huddled masses yearning to breathe free,
> The wretched refuse of your teeming shore.
> Send these, the homeless, tempest-tost to me,
> I lift my lamp beside the golden door!

It's no accident that white supremacists loathe those words. Trump advisor Stephen Miller railed against these powerful and iconic words, written by Emma Lazarus, that adorn the Statue of Liberty, saying the poem "is not part of the original Statue of Liberty."[5] Noted KKK Grand Wizard David Duke tweeted, "The poem cited initially had no connection to the Statue. It was added later by a Jewish Communist."[6] And it's easy to see why, among bigots, those words chafe. They speak of tolerance, of welcoming, of accepting the most downtrodden—and not from places like Norway but from those very countries Trump thinks of as "shit holes." Try as they might, the Trumpian white nationalist Right can't erase them from the story of America. We, as a nation, have been built on them.

And who cares *when* Lazarus's poem was added to the Statue of Liberty when Jefferson had long before spoken of tolerance in the Declaration of Independence. The words "Life, Liberty and the pursuit of Happiness" weren't defined in some narrow and bigoted way. If speaking Spanish to a same-sex partner makes someone happy, whose business is it to interfere?

None of that renders the concept of the American Dream obsolete. Quite the opposite, in fact. If someone works hard, is determined, and shows initiative, that person should have an equal chance to achieve success and prosperity, *irrespective* of gender, race, class, national origin, sexual orientation, or pretty much anything aside from simply being human. The American Dream is just as alive, relevant, and desirable today as it always has been. It must just be available to *all*.

We *are* a nation of risk-takers and dreamers and big thinkers who invented the telephone, the airplane, the personal computer, the internet, and the smartphone, and we will soon be sending people to Mars. Immigrants or their children have founded some of America's greatest companies, such as Amazon, Apple, AT&T, Boeing, GE, Google, Intel, Netflix, Pepsi, Pfizer, and Tesla. In fact, 216 of the companies in the Fortune 500 wouldn't exist without immigrants. This country is what it is *because* of those words on the Statue of Liberty. We may not have always lived up to their ideal. Our nation's history is tainted with the legacy of genocide, discrimination, and bigotry. We must still fully come to terms with our past in order to properly atone for it and then build a just and equitable future. We can't exclude anyone from this future—everyone's story must be told. But the *promise* of America is just as beautiful today as it has always been.

The American Dream claims that *anyone* seeking a better life can aspire to rise above their station, and *everyone* has an equal opportunity to become something better. That is our unifying narrative.

Our job, moving forward, in this world where Nazis march in American streets, mass murderers target marginalized communities, and white supremacists roam the White House, is to truly make the promise of that famous dream available to all.

Notes

1. Maya Oppenheim, "Steve Bannon Warns Trump the 'Anti-patriarchy Movement' Will Be Bigger Than the Tea Party," *Independent*, February 12, 2018, https://www.independent.co.uk/news/world/americas/us-politics/steve-bannon-trump-tea-party-anti-patriarchy-movement-times-up-bloomberg-breitbart-news-a8206426.html.

2. Congressional Record—House, vol. 152, pt. 11, p. 14796, July 18, 2006.

3. Amir Tibon, "White House Doubles Down on Holocaust Day Statement That Omitted Jews: 'We're Inclusive,'" *Haaretz*, January 29, 2017.

4. Bloomberg, "Donald Trump: There Is 'Blame on Both Sides' for Violent Clashes in Charlottesville," *Time*, August 15, 2017, http://time.com/4902159/donald-trump-there-is-blame-on-both-sides-for-violent-clashes-in-charlottesville/; Josh Dawsey, "Trump Derides Protections for Immigrants from 'Shithole' Countries," *Washington Post*, January 12, 2018; Tal Kopan, "What Donald Trump Has Said about Mexico and Vice Versa," CNN, August 31, 2016, https://www.cnn.com/2016/08/31/politics/donald-trump-mexico-statements/index.html.

5. Russell Contreras, "Stephen Miller Dismisses Statue of Liberty Poem," *U.S. News & World Report*, August 2, 2017.

6. David Duke on Twitter, January 31, 2017, https://twitter.com/drdavidduke/status/826526645582438403.

11

Foot-Voting Nation

ILYA SOMIN

I n an 1869 speech titled "Our Composite Nationality," the great African American abolitionist and political leader Frederick Douglass took white Americans to task for their growing hostility to Chinese immigration:

> I submit that this question of Chinese immigration should be settled upon higher principles than those of a cold and selfish expediency.
>
> There are such things in the world as human rights. They rest upon no conventional foundation, but are external, universal, and indestructible. Among these, is the right of locomotion; the right of migration; the right which belongs to no particular race, but belongs alike to all and to all alike. It is the right you assert by staying here, and your fathers asserted by coming here. It is this great right that I assert for the Chinese and Japanese, and for all other varieties of men equally with yourselves, now and forever.[1]

Elsewhere in the same speech, Douglass compared "repugnance to the presence and influence of foreigners" to "chattel slavery" and "prejudice of race and color."[2] It is no accident that Douglass, who first became famous because of his escape from slavery and work as an abolitionist, saw parallels between that institution and laws barring immigration. Both restricted "locomotion" and "the right of migration" on the basis of arbitrary circumstances of birth—in one case, race, in the other, geography.

In his early career, Douglass eloquently contended that slaves should be allowed to leave the authority of their masters. In the 1880s, after the rise of early segregation laws and other forms of repression deprived southern blacks of much of the freedom they hoped to gain after the Civil War, he argued that internal migration could help alleviate their oppression. In 1886 he said that "*diffusion* is the true policy for the colored people of the South," that as many blacks as possible should be encouraged to move to "parts of the country where their civil and political rights are better protected than at present they can be at the South," and that "a million of dollars devoted to this purpose [of assisting black migration out of the South] would do more for the colored people of the South than the same amount expended in any other way."[3]

Few have understood the importance of "the right of migration"—both internal and international—as fully as Douglass did. The combined impact of the two is a central feature of the American experiment and its relative success. Their denial—of which slavery was the most extreme form—has contributed to many of its greatest failures.

Democracy and ballot box voting have often been held up as central elements of the American political tradition. Less emphasis has been placed on the centrality of "voting with your feet." Yet in many ways, it is an even more fundamental and distinctive feature of American politics than electoral democracy.

Many nations have had democratic governments, and democratic institutions long predate the founding of the United States, tracing their origins to ancient Greece. In modern times, a good many political systems have been more democratic than the United States in the sense of giving greater power to political majorities. The U.S. Constitution is—depending on your point of view—either celebrated or notorious for its many counter-majoritarian elements, such as a Senate that gives hugely disproportionate weight to small states and very strong judicial review wielded by judges appointed for life.[4] By contrast, few if any other nations have been so heavily influenced by "foot voting" through both internal and international migration. Both immigration and internal migration between states are, in most cases, forms of foot voting: the use of mobility to choose which government policies one wishes to live under.

Many have noted the importance of immigration to the American experience. The crucial role of federalism and internal migration between jurisdictions has also attracted a great deal of attention. But few if any have tried to combine the two in a unified framework for understanding America.

A good many nations have experienced extensive foot voting through immigration. Others have had extensive internal migration between subnational jurisdictions. But none, perhaps, have been as heavily shaped by the combination of these two forces as America has. The nation's success is, to a very large extent, the product of the interaction between these two types of foot voting.

The first section of this chapter provides a brief overview of the role of immigration in the American political tradition, a role that has deep roots going back to the time of the Founding. The second focuses on internal foot voting. Unlike immigration, the importance of the latter was not well understood by the Founding Fathers. They nonetheless designed a political system that facilitated it in crucial ways, and it has had a profound impact since. Finally, the third part considers the continuing importance of foot voting in modern times, as well as emerging threats to its effectiveness, in the form of nationalist movements hostile to immigration and regulatory barriers that impede internal foot voting.

Immigration

The Founding Fathers early on recognized the importance of foot voting through immigration as a key feature of their society and a crucial element in the success of the new nation. In his famous 1774 essay, *A Summary View of the Rights of British America*, Thomas Jefferson noted that "our ancestors, before their emigration to America, were the free inhabitants of the British dominions in Europe, and possessed a right which nature has given to all men, of departing from the country in which chance, not choice, has placed them, of going in quest of new habitations, and of there establishing new societies, under such laws and regulations as to them shall seem most likely to promote public happiness."[5]

Two year later, one of the charges Jefferson leveled against King George III in the Declaration of Independence was that "he has endeavored to prevent the population of these states; for that purpose obstructing the laws for naturalization of foreigners; *refusing to pass others to encourage their migration hither.*"[6] The Founding Fathers and other early American leaders expected extensive immigration. With the brief exception of the controversial Alien Acts of 1798, the federal government maintained a policy of open migration intended to attract immigrants to what both Americans and many Europeans saw as a land of refuge from the oppression of the Old World.[7]

Between 1820 and 1924 some thirty-six million immigrants arrived in the United States.[8] The vast bulk of the American population consists of their descendants. Under federal law, immigration from around the world was almost completely unconstrained until the Chinese Exclusion Act of 1882, and immigration from Europe remained so until the 1920s.[9] The Immigration Act of 1924, driven by rising nativist sentiment, greatly curtailed immigration for the next forty years by adopting strict national quotas favoring Northern and Western European nations.[10] But the Immigration Act of 1965 once again greatly liberalized immigration, if not to the near "open borders" extent of the pre-1924 era.[11] The result has been another major expansion of immigration from many parts of the world. Today, over 13 percent of the American population consists of foreign-born immigrants, up from about 5 percent in 1960.[12]

The reasons why so many immigrants have come to the United States over the last two centuries vary greatly. But foot voting in favor of a better political system with more favorable government policies has been a major factor. Many of the nineteenth-century immigrants came to the United States in search of religious and ethnic toleration, as in the case of Jews fleeing czarist Russia, Irish Catholics fleeing Britain, and many others. Other nineteenth-century migrants were political dissenters, including many who fled in the aftermath of the suppression of liberal revolutions in Europe in 1848.

The same, of course, is true of numerous modern immigrants, who also include many fleeing ethnic and religious persecution or political repression. The cases of refugees from Nazism, Cubans, Soviet Jews, Vietnamese "boat people," and, most recently, Syrian refugees fleeing oppression by ISIS and the regime of Bashar Assad are obvious examples.

Even many "economic" migrants choose the United States for policy-related reasons. Economic opportunity is to a large extent the product of government policy, and the relative lack of opportunity in many immigrants' homelands was heavily determined by the policies of the regimes in power there. This, too, is true of both nineteenth- and early twentieth-century immigrants and those of today. What we refer to as "economic" migration is very often also a form of political foot voting.

Internal Foot Voting

The role of internal foot voting in American history is almost as significant as that of international migration, though its centrality may be less often recognized. Unlike immigration, domestic foot voting was not much considered by the Founding Fathers, who gave it little, if any, attention in their otherwise extensive writings on federalism. But by designing a federal system with a high degree of decentralization and room for interjurisdictional competition, they nonetheless created a political system with many opportunities for foot voting.[13] The most famous example is, of course, westward migration to the frontier in the nineteenth century, in which millions moved west to settle the vast territories acquired in the 1803 Louisiana Purchase, the Mexican War of 1846–47, and other land acquisitions.

But the United States also has an extensive history of other forms of internal foot voting, most notably, that by ethnic and religious minorities seeking more tolerant jurisdictions. The best-known case is, of course, the migration of African Americans from the South to other parts of the country beginning in the late nineteenth century and extending through the middle of the twentieth. Between approximately 1880 and 1920, over a million southern-born African Americans migrated to the North or the West.[14] By 1920 such migrants accounted for some 10 percent of the total black population of the United States, which then stood at 10.4 million.[15] There was an even larger black migration from south to north in the years immediately following World War II.[16] A 1917 NAACP publication claimed that migration to the North was "the most effective protest against Southern lynching, lawlessness, and general deviltry."[17]

Other examples include the movement of the Mormons to Utah, fleeing persecution in the eastern states, and, in more modern times, the movement of gays and lesbians to relatively tolerant cities and states with more favorable policies.[18]

As with international migration, much internal migration is driven by economic factors, such as the search for job opportunities and affordable housing. But, again like international migration, much internal economic migration has a crucial political dimension. State and local government policies on such issues as zoning, labor market regulation, and taxation have a major impact on the economic factors that incentivize internal migration. As a result, interjurisdictional migration motivated by "economic" concerns is often a form of political foot voting.[19]

This was even to an important degree true of westward migration during the "frontier" era. In addition to free or cheap land and other narrowly "economic" opportunities, western territories also often offered new forms of governance that were more flexible and tolerant than those in the East. Contrary to the mythology of the "Wild West," these institutions often kept order and provided public goods better than their eastern counterparts.[20] Many western territorial and state governments also offered greater tolerance and a measure of equality to groups that were marginalized or excluded elsewhere. In order to attract more female settlers, for example, western governments were the first to give women the right to vote, beginning with the then Wyoming Territory in 1869.[21]

Internal foot voting remains a major aspect of American society today. Some 43 percent of Americans have made at least one interstate move in their lifetime, and 63 percent have made a move of some kind, including within a state.[22]

In recent decades, foot voting often occurs not only between conventional political jurisdictions but also between private planned communities. Some sixty million Americans now live in such private communities, many of which provide security, environmental amenities, and many other services traditionally associated with local governments.[23] Private communities can often offer a wider range of choice and lower moving costs to potential foot voters than traditional local and state governments can.[24]

Both public jurisdictions and private communities often compete for residents in order to increase property value and attract revenue. This, in turn, expands foot-voting opportunities and increases the range of choice available to potential migrants.

As with immigration, internal foot voting has created enormous gains, both economic and otherwise. On the economic side, it has enabled millions to move to areas where they could be more productive and achieve a higher standard of living. These gains are so great as to be virtually incalculable.

Even more difficult to measure are the "noneconomic" benefits, such as those achieved by African Americans and Mormons who escaped state-sponsored oppression, women who moved to more egalitarian jurisdictions in the nineteenth-century West, and gays and lesbians who moved to areas where homophobia was less prevalent. Yet these gains, too, have been great indeed.

In addition to its more conventional economic and other benefits, foot voting has also served as an important mechanism for facilitating political freedom—a valuable supplement to conventional ballot box voting. As a mechanism for exercising political choice, ballot box voting has two important shortcomings: the individual voter has very little chance of making a decisive choice, and for that very reason, he or she has strong incentives to make poorly informed decisions.[25]

In most elections, an individual voter has only an infinitesimal chance of making a decisive difference to the outcome.[26] As a result, his or her influence over the government policies she must live under is minimal. A form of freedom where one's choices have almost no chance of making a difference has, at the very least, serious limitations. It does not accord well with either intuitive notions of what it means to be free or more analytically sophisticated conceptions of political freedom developed by political theorists.[27]

The insignificance of the individual vote also diminishes the likelihood of making a well-informed choice. Because there is so little probability that their choices will make a difference, most voters have strong incentives to be "rationally ignorant"—to devote little or no time and effort to acquiring political knowledge.[28] Decades of survey data do in fact reveal that most voters have low levels of political knowledge and often make decisions based on ignorance, crude biases, and "shortcuts."[29] To the extent we believe that meaningful political freedom requires informed choice, this should be deeply troubling.

By contrast, foot voters are able to make decisive choices. At least in most cases, their decisions about where to live do indeed make a difference to the policies they will have to live under. As a result, they also tend to seek out more information and analyze it more objectively than ballot box voters do.[30] American history shows that foot voters often effectively find information and use it wisely even under highly adverse conditions, such as those faced by African Americans fleeing the Jim Crow era South and poor immigrants who chose to come to the United States from Europe and Asia in the nineteenth century.[31]

The Future of Foot Voting in America

While foot voting is a central part of the American story and has helped create enormous benefits, it has also often generated political backlash. At many points in the nineteenth and early twentieth centuries, immigration helped spawn powerful nativist movements, such as the Know-Nothings of the 1850s, racist backlash against Chinese immigration in the 1870s and 1880s, and the effort to curb migration that ultimately culminated in the highly restrictive Immigration Act of 1924.[32] Donald Trump's victory in the 2016 election after a campaign focused on hostility to immigration may be the start of another major period of nativist backlash. Whether the administration succeeds in imposing extensive long-term reductions in immigration remains to be seen. But at least for the moment, opposition to immigration is a central feature of right-of-center politics in the United States, as in many European countries. That opposition is not limited to illegal migration but also seeks to radically reduce legal immigration.[33]

Opposition to internal migration has also been common in American history. Well-known examples include hostility to African Americans moving into previously all-white neighborhoods and "exclusionary zoning" regulations intended to keep out racial minorities and the poor.[34]

Much of the opposition to immigration and domestic foot voting has been rooted in racial and ethnic prejudice and simple ignorance.[35] During the 2016 election, for example, Donald Trump notoriously exploited public ignorance about immigration and crime rates, among other issues, falsely claiming that immigration increases crime, whereas the opposite is in fact the case.[36] But some of the opposition has also been based on more defensible concerns about assimilation, potential political disruption, and burdens on the welfare state, among other considerations.[37]

The recent political backlash against immigration has coincided with a less visible but also extensive expansion of barriers to internal foot voting. Restrictive zoning in major cities such as New York and San Francisco has artificially inflated the cost of housing and locked millions of the poor and disadvantaged out of areas where they could otherwise find valuable job opportunities.[38] State-based occupational licensing has also become a formidable barrier to movement, cutting off potential migrants from important job opportunities.[39]

Breaking down barriers to immigration and internal foot voting could create enormous benefits. A recent study by the National Bureau of Economic Research estimates that reducing restrictive zoning rules to the level that prevails in the median city would increase GDP by as much as 9.5 percent by enabling more workers to move to areas with greater opportunity.[40] Reducing obstacles to international migration could have even larger benefits.

Economists estimate that allowing free migration throughout the world would likely double world GDP, with much of that benefit concentrated in the United States.[41] Even more modest increases in mobility could still produce major benefits, including many that are not narrowly "economic" in nature.[42]

Efforts to expand foot voting must, as much as possible, address potential costs and negative side effects. I cannot address these issues in detail here, but a brief discussion is in order.

Many claimed negative side effects of migration and foot voting are greatly overstated. To take one oft-discussed example, the available data indicate that increased immigration does not lead to increases in welfare spending; therefore, concerns about overburdening the welfare state are largely misplaced.[43] Immigrants to the United States have a much lower crime rate than native-born citizens do, thereby undercutting claims that immigration increases the crime rate.[44]

Where migration does cause genuine problems, it is often possible to address them by utilizing "keyhole solutions" that reduce harm without restricting mobility.[45] For example, if immigration does impose excessive burdens on the welfare state, the United States could reduce welfare benefits to immigrants.[46]

If all else fails, we can mitigate the negative effects of expanded foot voting by tapping some of the vast wealth created by migration itself. For example, if migrant labor reduces wages for local labor and we conclude that the latter is entitled to compensation, then that compensation can be provided by taxing migrants or their customers and employers and redistributing the revenue to displaced workers.[47]

Excluding migrants from welfare benefits or imposing discriminatory taxation on them may be unjust. I do not consider such policies to be anywhere close to ideal. But they inflict less harm and injustice than excluding potential migrants from the United States entirely or locking internal foot voters out of more desirable areas.

• • •

Perhaps more than any other major nation, the United States is defined by its history of foot voting. The nation would not have achieved more than a fraction of its enormous wealth and power without it. More importantly, foot voting has enabled many millions of people to find greater freedom, prosperity, and happiness.

If, as President Trump says, we seek to make America great again, we would do well to build on and expand the tradition of foot voting that did so much to make America great in the first place.

Notes

1. Frederick Douglass, "Our Composite Nationality: An Address Delivered in Boston, Massachusetts, December 7, 1869," in *The Frederick Douglass Papers: Series One: Speeches, Debates and Interviews*, ed. John Blassingame and John McKivigan (New Haven CT: Yale University Press, 1991), 4:240–59, 252.

2. Douglass, "Our Composite Nationality," 250–51.

3. Frederick Douglass, *Selected Speeches and Writings*, ed. Philip S. Foner and Yuval Taylor (1886; Chicago: Lawrence Hill Books, 1999), 702.

4. For a highly critical analysis of these countermajoritarian tendencies, see Sanford M. Levinson, *Our Undemocratic Constitution* (Princeton NJ: Princeton University Press, 2006).

5. Thomas Jefferson, *A Summary View of the Rights of British America, Set Forth in Some Resolutions Intended for the Inspection of the Present Delegates of the People of Virginia. Now in Convention. By a Native, and Member of the House of Burgesses* (Williamsburg VA: Printed by Clementina Rind, [1774]).

6. Declaration of Independence, para. 9 (U.S. 1776), emphasis added.

7. See generally Marilyn C. Baseler, *"Asylum for Mankind": America 1607–1800* (Ithaca NY: Cornell University Press, 1998), chaps. 4–8. Some constraints on immigration were, however, imposed by state governments during this era. See Gerald Neuman, "The Lost Century of American Immigration Law, 1776–1875," *Columbia Law Review* 93 (1993): 833.

8. Roger V. Daniels, *Coming to America: A History of Immigration and Ethnicity in American Life*, 2nd ed. (New York: Perennial, 2002), 124.

9. Daniels, *Coming to America*, 245–46 and chap. 10.

10. Daniels, *Coming to America*, chap. 11.

11. For an overview of the 1965 act and its consequences, see Tom Gjelten, *A Nation of Nations: A Great American Immigration Story* (New York: Simon & Schuster, 2015), esp. chap. 10.

12. Pew Research Center, "Modern Immigration Wave Brings 59 Million to U.S., Driving Population Growth and Change Through 2065," September 28, 2015, http://assets.pewresearch.org/wp-content/uploads/sites/7/2015/09/2015-09-28_modern-immigration-wave_REPORT.pdf.

13. For a detailed exposition of the ways in which the founding design of American federalism facilitates interjurisdictional competition and choice,

see Michael S. Greve, *The Upside-Down Constitution* (Cambridge MA: Harvard University Press, 2012), chaps. 1–3.

14. Daniel M. Johnson and Rex R. Campbell, *Black Migration in America: A Social Demographic History* (Durham NC: Duke University Press, 1981), 74–75.

15. Johnson and Campbell, *Black Migration*, 77.

16. Johnson and Campbell, *Black Migration*, 114–23.

17. Quoted in Michael J. Klarman, *From Jim Crow to Civil Rights: The Supreme Court and the Struggle for Racial Equality* (New York: Oxford University Press, 2004), 164.

18. See Stephen Clark, "Progressive Federalism? A Gay Liberationist Perspective," *Albany Law Review* 66 (2003): 719–57.

19. For a more detailed discussion of this point, see Ilya Somin, *Democracy and Political Ignorance: Why Smaller Government Is Smarter*, 2nd ed. (Stanford CA: Stanford University Press, 2016), 166–67.

20. See Terry Anderson and Peter J. Hill, *The Not So Wild, Wild West: Property Rights on the Frontier* (Stanford CA: Stanford University Press, 2004).

21. See, for example, Akhil Reed Amar, *The Law of the Land: A Grand Tour of Our Constitutional Republic* (New York: Basic Books, 2015), 227; T. A. Larson, "Woman Suffrage in Wyoming," *Pacific Northwest Quarterly* 56 (1965): 57–66.

22. Somin, *Democracy and Political Ignorance*, 166.

23. Edward Peter Stringham, *Private Governance: Creating Order in Economic and Social Life* (New York: Oxford University Press, 2015), 131; Robert Nelson, *Private Neighborhoods and the Transformation of Local Government* (Washington DC: Urban Institute, 2005).

24. See Somin, *Democracy and Political Ignorance*, 157–59; and Ilya Somin, "Foot Voting, Federalism, and Political Freedom," in *Nomos: Federalism and Subsidiarity*, ed. James Fleming and Jacob Levy (New York: New York University Press, 2014).

25. See Somin, "Foot Voting, Federalism, and Political Freedom"; and Ilya Somin, "Foot Voting vs. Ballot Box Voting: Why Voting with Your Feet Is Crucial to Political Freedom," *European Political Science* (forthcoming).

26. See, for example, Somin, *Democracy and Political Ignorance*, chap. 3.

27. On the latter point, see Somin, "Foot Voting vs. Ballot Box Voting."

28. For the classic elaboration of the theory of rational voter ignorance, see Anthony Downs, *An Economic Theory of Democracy* (New York: Harper & Row, 1957), chap. 13. For a recent overview, see Somin, *Democracy and Political Ignorance*, chap. 3.

29. For recent summaries of the evidence, see Somin, *Democracy and Political Ignorance*, chap. 1; Jason Brennan, *Against Democracy* (Princeton NJ: Princeton University Press, 2016); Christopher Achen and Larry Bartels, *Democracy for Realists: Why Elections Do Not Produce Responsive Government* (Princeton NJ: Princeton University Press, 2016); and Rick Shenkman,

Just How Stupid Are We? Facing the Truth about the American Voter (New York: Basic Books, 2008).

30. For extensive analysis of relevant evidence, see Somin, *Democracy and Political Ignorance*, chap. 5.

31. Somin, *Democracy and Political Ignorance*, 148–51.

32. See, for example, Daniels, *Coming to America*, 241–47 and chap. 10; John Higham, *Strangers in the Land: Patterns of American Nativism, 1860–1925* (New York: Athenaeum, 1969).

33. For example, Trump and many Republican members of Congress have endorsed the RAISE Act, which would cut legal immigration in half. See Ilya Somin, "Trump's Cruel and Counterproductive Effort to Slash Legal Immigration," Volokh Conspiracy, *Washington Post*, August 3, 2017, https:// www.washingtonpost.com/news/volokh-conspiracy/wp/2017/08/03/trumps -cruel-and-counterproductive-effort-to-slash-legal-immigration/?utm_term =.2457034a3f01.

34. See generally Richard Rothstein, *The Color of Law: A Forgotten History of How Our Government Segregated America* (New York: Norton, 2017); Sonia Hirt, *Zoned in the USA: The Origins and Implications of American Land-Use Regulation* (Ithaca NY: Cornell University Press, 2014); William A. Fischel, "An Economic History of Zoning and a Cure for Its Exclusionary Effects," *Urban Studies* 41 (2004): 317–40.

35. Opposition to immigration in both the United States and Europe is closely correlated with ignorance about the number of immigrants and their impact and xenophobic attitudes toward foreigners. For a detailed overview of the evidence, see Jens Hainmueller and Daniel J. Hopkins, "Public Attitudes towards Immigration," *Annual Review of Political Science* 17 (2014): 224–49, esp. 224–35. On the impact of economic ignorance on opposition to immigration, see, for example, Bryan Caplan, *The Myth of the Rational Voter: Why Democracies Choose Bad Policies* (Princeton NJ: Princeton University Press, 2007), 38–39, 58–59.

36. See Ilya Somin, "Political Ignorance Haunts 2016 Campaign," CNN, May 12, 2016, https://www.cnn.com/2016/05/12/opinions/political-ignorance -somin/index.html.

37. For examples of such arguments, see Samuel P. Huntington, *Who Are We? The Challenges to America's National Identity* (New York: Simon & Schuster, 2004); Philip Cafaro, *How Many Is Too Many? The Progressive Argument for Reducing Immigration into the United States* (Chicago: University of Chicago Press, 2014).

38. For recent overviews of the evidence, see, for example, David Schleicher, "Stuck! The Law and the Economics of Residential Stability," *Yale Law Journal* 127 (2018): 78–154; and Edward Glaeser, "Reforming Land Use Regulations," Brookings Institution, April 24, 2017, https://www.brookings.edu /research/reforming-land-use-regulations/amp.

39. See Ilya Somin, "Moving Vans More Powerful Than Ballot Boxes," *USA Today*, October 18, 2016, www.usatoday.com/story/opinion/2016/10/18/mobility-zoning-licensing-voting-minorities-column/91990486/.

40. See Chang Tai-Hsieh and Enrico Moretti, "Housing Constraints and Spatial Misallocation," NBER Working Paper No. 21154 (2015), http://www.nber.org/papers/w21154. For an overview of the evidence, see Glaeser, "Reforming Land Use Regulations."

41. On the effect of migration on world GDP, see Michael Clemens, "Economics and Emigration: Trillion Dollar Bills Left on the Sidewalk?," *Journal of Economic Perspectives* 25 (2011): 83–106.

42. For a more detailed discussion, see Ilya Somin, "Foot Voting, Decentralization, and Development," *Minnesota Law Review* 102 (2018): 1649–70.

43. See, for example, Alex Nowrasteh and Zac Gochenour, "The Political Externalities of Immigration: Evidence from the United States," Cato Institute Working Paper, January 2014, http://object.cato.org/sites/cato.org/files/pubs/pdf/working-paper-14–3.pdf (evidence from American states); Alberto Alesina and Edward L. Glaeser, *Fighting Poverty in the US and Europe: A World of Difference* (New York: Oxford University Press, 2004) (evidence indicating that European nations with greater immigration actually have lower welfare spending than those with more).

44. For a review of the relevant studies and evidence, see Mary Waters and Marisa Gerstein Pineau, *The Integration of Immigrants into American Society* (Washington DC: National Academy of Sciences, 2015), 326–32.

45. For examples of such proposals, see Bryan Caplan, "Why Should We Restrict Immigration?," *Cato Journal* 32 (2012): 5–21. I present others in Somin, *Free to Move: Foot Voting and Political Freedom* (Oxford University Press, forthcoming).

46. Compare Martin Ruhs, *The Cost of Rights: Regulating International Labor Migration* (Princeton NJ: Princeton University Press, 2014) (documenting how limiting the welfare rights of labor migrants can enable increased migration).

47. For this idea, see Caplan, "Why Should We Restrict Immigration?"

12

Transatlantic Perspectives

SPENCER P. BOYER

F ew disagree that the United States is more politically and
culturally divided today than at any point since the Vietnam
War, with ample evidence of the internal divide abound-
ing. One could point to startling statistics confirming how differently Democrats and Republicans view the current political
environment—especially President Donald J. Trump's brand of
leadership—and the extent to which we distrust the motives of
those with whom we disagree.[1]

One could also show how Americans self-segregate ideologi-
cally, creating redder red states and bluer blue ones. Most Americans have just a few or no friends from the opposing party.[2]
Gerrymandering certainly compounds political divisions, creating unnaturally safe districts for some of the most partisan
and extreme politicians in Congress, spurring ongoing judicial
review of constitutionality.

These telltale signs of a fractured United States, however,
raise a more fundamental question: What does it mean to be an
American almost two decades into the twenty-first century? At
the core of these extreme U.S. political and cultural divisions
rages a struggle to appropriate and define the term "American."

Just a few years ago, it seemed as though America was moving toward a more inclusive and expansive concept than we had
ever seen before. For many, the election of Barack Obama—the
first person of color to win the presidency—signaled a watershed
moment in America's long, tortuous racial history. It appeared
that the American people had collectively embraced the notion

that one could have a multicultural and multiethnic background and still be considered a quintessential American, holding the highest office in the land. The world cheered as the United States finally seemed to be living up to the ideals of tolerance and acceptance it had championed for so long. Global sentiments about the desirability of U.S. leadership soared.[3] But that was then.

Times have changed quickly, and a new soul-searching has begun. The 2016 presidential campaign and subsequent presidency of Mr. Trump disabused even the most hopeful of the idea that we have crossed over into a postracial America in which significant tension rooted in perceived ethnic and religious differences are twentieth-century relics. Instead of debating how best to deepen integration of minority groups, we have been divided over whether travel bans on individuals coming from certain Muslim majority countries are necessary for security—or are even constitutional. Instead of a growing consensus about the value of immigration and diversity, Mr. Trump's vision of a physical wall on our southern border and a significant reduction in legal immigration has found fertile ground in many quarters of the country. Far Right populism and ethnic nationalism in the United States have become more mainstream as political leaders have openly courted race-based grievance and put forward "outsiders" as the primary reason for economic and other societal challenges in both rural and urban communities.

Fortunately, the most powerful American unifying theme of the late twentieth and early twenty-first centuries—*a respect for and an acceptance of multiple identities*—remains one of our greatest strengths. The difficult American journey from slavery to Jim Crow era segregation to the current period, where "hyphenated Americans" are commonplace and uncontroversial, has created something culturally unique in modern society.

Other Western democracies have, of course, also struggled for decades with how to integrate millions of immigrants, with recent migration pressures in Europe adding to the workload. But while there are similar challenges on both sides of the Atlantic, the fact that the United States has a collective theme built upon a layered, dynamic, and growing concept of "us" will likely be the country's glue during these politically and culturally explosive times and could be a guide for the future both here and abroad.

• • •

When debating whether there is a unifying American story at the moment, it would certainly be justifiable to say "absolutely not." On the surface, Americans appear to be moving farther apart and down tribal lines. American cultural, racial, and ethnic divisions that exploded during the 2016 presidential campaign—and were successfully exploited by some within the Trump campaign and the Kremlin, disinformation trolls and other Russian proxies, and independent actors intent on sowing chaos—paint a dark picture of a country at war with itself.[4]

This tension can be found in the recent, robust, activist response to alleged police misconduct involving African Americans throughout the country and was epitomized in 2017 in Charlottesville, Virginia, when white supremacist demonstrators clashed with counterprotestors, leaving a young woman dead. President Trump's response—equating the behavior of the white supremacists with the counterprotestors—caused an outcry among many.

Yet the current turmoil must be placed in context. Despite today's gulf, the United States has arguably achieved a deeper and more widespread acceptance of differences and greater success in codifying nondiscrimination practices than a number of its Western counterparts. Civil rights era legislation and experiences that ended legal segregation in the public realm—and their enforcement through individual court challenges and robust class-action lawsuits by minorities in subsequent years—have helped shape, over time, a broader public acceptance of America's multicultural identity. The road there, however, has been long.[5]

In this immigrant nation, the distinction between "insiders" and "outsiders" has always been fluid, dynamic, and complex. While every group arriving in the United States has had its unique challenges, nineteenth- and twentieth-century immigrants from Anglo-Saxon Protestant countries in Western Europe were, understandably, more easily incorporated into the American mainstream than those from countries more distinct and diverse in terms of religion, race, and ethnicity. The view of "us," however, has evolved, allowing for an expanded American identity.

Past societal barriers to acceptance were often quite different from those of today. Polish, Italian, and Irish Catholic migrants in the mid- to late nineteenth century were heavily discriminated against in housing, employment, and other realms of American life based in part on security concerns rooted in stereotypes about aggressiveness and inferiority. During World War II, well over half a million Italians were branded as potential "enemy aliens" and stripped of their privacy rights. Hundreds were sent to internment camps.[6] And as recently as 1960, when John F. Kennedy made his historic run, the world doubted whether a Catholic could be elected president.

Today's European American subgroups, however, are now largely seen as just part of a wider European American majority. Ethnic enclaves and residential and social segregation by choice still exist throughout the country. However, barriers to the integration of white Europeans or their descendants into the mainstream based solely on ancestral origin or being a non-Protestant Christian have all but vanished in twenty-first-century America.

For African Americans and immigrants of color from other parts of the world, the integration experience has clearly been much different. And among those of color, the African American experience has, of course, been without parallel. Despite the challenges of certain European American immigrants, for most of American history, race and color distinctions, as opposed to differences rooted in other areas, have been at the leading edge of determining how local, state, and federal officials legally classified and treated U.S. citizens and residents.

Although formal barriers to integration were dismantled through the Supreme Court's 1954 *Brown v. Board of Education* decision and subsequent civil rights legislation that uprooted institutionalized segregation in housing, employment, education, and public facilities, America nevertheless allowed slavery and Jim Crow laws for generations, which profoundly impacted black integration efforts.

Significant disparities in wealth, income, and education between African Americans and white Americans, as well as the disproportionate number of blacks who are in the criminal justice system, are indicators that race still plays a role in social and professional mobility in America. African American boys raised in the United States, even in the wealthiest families and living in upper-middle-class neighborhoods, still earn less in adulthood than Caucasian boys with similar backgrounds.[7]

At the same time, traditional color lines changed dramatically in the United States with the influx of Latino and Asian immigrants over the past few decades, along with the rapid growth of a self-defined multiracial population. Latinos are now the largest minority group in the country—overtaking African Americans in the past decade—reaching 18 percent of the U.S. population.[8] Asians are the next fastest growing minority group, having reached approximately 6 percent of the population. In 2000 approximately 2 percent of Americans identified themselves as multiracial.[9] By 2050 the National Academy of Sciences predicts that the multiracial population could rise to over 20 percent. By 2045 whites will no longer be the majority population in the United States.[10]

Thus, the former color divides—codified and pervasive for much of America's existence—have become messier as the United States has diversified. As a result, Americans now view themselves in more complex ways. The multicultural past and present have shaped a unique conception of an American story or identity that acknowledges that one can be a "real" American regardless of how one looks and regardless of who one's ancestors were. In short, one can belong to one or more cultural groups and still be an unquestioned American.

• • •

The 2016 U.S. presidential election and deep divisions about what this historical moment means are making many question whether the progress the country seemed to have made away from identity politics and toward the acceptance of a multicultural America was as strong as it seemed. Fears and resentments are being expressed in a more powerful way than many imagined just a few years ago, with tens of millions of Americans drawn to narratives, especially concerning immigration, that have traditionally been viewed as on the fringes.

In many ways, the electorate is more polarized today regarding the definition of American identity and the value of diversity—often breaking along socioeconomic, educational, and ethnic lines—than at any time in recent memory. There are certainly many causes of this polarization, including economic anxiety and displacement; a perceived loss of values and a way of life with continued strong immigration; and a fear of immigrant crime and foreign terrorism, often stoked by exaggerated claims about the threat. Trump voters, for example, were likelier than others to believe that undocumented immigrants are more prone to commit serious crimes than American citizens, despite evidence to the contrary.[11]

The result is that for many Americans, immigration and demographic change pose a visible and direct threat to established concepts of nation, identity, and previous social hierarchies—a narrative that has been aggressively stoked by certain high-level politicians and proxies over the past couple of years.

• • •

Europe's experience with identity at both the national and supranational levels has been significantly different, with most EU member states grappling with diversity issues for a much briefer period of time. While countries such as France, the United Kingdom, and the Netherlands had significant histories as colonial powers in the developing world and received immigrants in the early to mid-nineteenth century, most European countries are considered fairly "new" immigrant nations as compared to the United States, Canada, or Australia.

Substantial migrations from European former colonies, especially British, French, and Belgian colonies in Africa and Asia, began arriving on the Continent in the period following World War II. Sizable numbers of guest workers from Turkey, Yugoslavia, and poorer southern European countries followed, moving north and west in the 1960s and 1970s.[12] Until this time, most European societies correctly viewed themselves as being fundamentally homogeneous.

There was little debate about what it meant to be Swedish, German, French, or Italian—it was primarily a matter of ancestry and ethnic heritage. Today, however, the demographics of Europe are fundamentally different from what they were four or five decades ago, forcing European societies to grapple with issues of self-perception and integration in ways they have never had to before. The so-called temporary guest workers of the mid-twentieth century became permanent fixtures within European populations after most Western European countries ended importation of labor during the oil crises of the early to mid-1970s.[13] Thousands never returned to their home countries and often brought family to join them in Europe. Host countries pledged to integrate the foreign workers who remained while discouraging them from staying. Voluntary repatriation policies were largely unsuccessful.[14]

As of early 2017, there were nearly thirty-seven million people born outside of the EU living in EU countries, while more than twenty million people were living in an EU country different from the one they were born in.[15] Countries such as Germany, the UK, France, Sweden, Denmark, Austria, and the Netherlands have now established themselves as countries of immigration, with others quickly joining those ranks. In the process, the face of Europe has changed, resulting in soul-searching across the continent about what it actually means to be European. Is it solely about citizenship? Does ethnic ancestry or religion matter? Can one truly be Czech or German and look Turkish or Algerian? Should dual nationalities or multiple identifications be accepted in society?

• • •

Irregular migration has, of course, thrown fuel on the fire for those who were already concerned with legal immigration into Europe. While overall migration numbers are significantly down from the 2015 and 2016 surge—with the EU receiving 43 percent fewer asylum applications in 2017 than it did in 2016—southern European countries, especially Italy, continue to bear the brunt of migrant arrivals, and countries that took in hundreds of thousands, such as Germany, will be grappling with long-term integration challenges for years to come.[16]

Within a challenging regional political context, xenophobic forces across Europe find fertile ground in their efforts to exacerbate the issue. Whether discussing Sweden, France, Poland, Hungary, Belgium, Denmark, the Netherlands, Germany, or Italy, populist and extreme right-wing leaders and parties have been using irregular migration and immigration to fuel their movements, putting more mainstream parties on the defensive. The attitude toward migrants in many parts of Europe further soured over revelations that some terrorists were able to sneak into Europe with legitimate asylum seekers.

Furthermore, the cultural and historical backgrounds of some countries with no significant tradition of integrating large numbers of foreigners into the mainstream have also complicated the acceptance of migrants. The 2015 EU commitment to relocate 160,000 asylum seekers from Greece and Italy to other member states faced massive resistance in some parts of Central and Eastern Europe. Protecting Poland's religious homogeneity, for instance, seems to have been at the forefront of its migration policy. Other countries, such as Hungary, the Czech Republic, and Slovakia, also refused migrants for political and cultural reasons.

• • •

In addition to migration, a number of other causes contribute to a rise in populist and nationalist leaders in Europe today, but the resulting mindset still creates an atmosphere where an expansive definition of "us" is less popular. The drivers of European division include political parties, national leaders, and EU officials who continue to disagree on the proper functions and powers of the EU; a long-term increase in electoral volatility in Europe, which brings less durable national governments that strain at, if not reject, the kind of trade-offs that have been the cornerstone of EU policymaking; and the threat of Islamic extremism from the Middle East and Africa, which increasingly alarms publics while failing to generate support for a uniform response. Furthermore, a more belligerent Russia continues to use propaganda, disinformation, financial contributions, and other support to boost anti-EU and anti-U.S. parties.

New and often populist parties are taking advantage of the resulting public fear and dissatisfaction as well as the decline in ideological distance between the established Left and Right, harnessing that anxiety in a manner that bolsters anti-immigrant rhetoric and policy choices. Some parties, such as the Freedom Party in Austria, are dropping their former anti-Semitic positions and adopting pro-Israel platforms to broaden their appeal, focusing animosity toward Muslims in Europe instead.

• • •

So where does this leave us? What can we learn from each other's experiences in grappling with these forces that pull at the seams of our societies? What do these divisions mean for unifying national or Western themes?

Perhaps the most important lesson is how many similarities there are between right-wing populist movements in Europe and the recent political groundswell in the United States and thus in the shared challenge for those who have concerns with our direction. These core narratives focus on immigrants and migrants taking jobs, Muslims and other newcomers threatening security, political correctness undermining the ability to speak one's mind, supposed mainstream media lying, and the establishment selling out the working class in the service of the wealthy elite.

In addition, on both sides of the Atlantic, an incomplete economic account tries to explain nationalism and populism as arising with growing inequality and social exclusion. The fact that populist, authoritarian leaders arose in several affluent societies with educated populations and generous welfare states provides evidence of a stronger driver: cultural backlash against changes in social values. In the end, the greatest impact can often occur from manipulating perceptions of change for communities and individuals for political advantage (as opposed to objective economic indicators).

There is a great deal of transatlantic work to do in figuring out how to better balance harnessing the diversity and change needed for economic and social growth—while at the same time reaching those who feel left behind by change—in order to create an environment where closed borders and deportation are less attractive policy prescriptions. The unique American experience, with its emphasis on multiple identities being a fundamental part of the national narrative, could go a long way in helping inform a broader transatlantic dialogue on inclusion for everyone, newcomers and native born alike.

Notes

1. See Bruce Stokes, "How Americans See Themselves and the World in Trump Era," Pew Research Center, April 2018.

2. Pew Research Center Survey, conducted June 8–18, 2017.

3. Fran Newport and Andrew Dugan, "5 Ways America Changed during the Obama Years," Gallup Polling Matters, January 27, 2017, https://news .gallup.com/opinion/polling-matters/203123/america-changed-during-obama -years.aspx.

4. See Alina Polyakova and Spencer P. Boyer, "The Future of Political Warfare: Russia the West, and the Coming Age of Global Digital Competition," Brookings Institution, March 2018, https://www.brookings.edu/research/the -future-of-political-warfare-russia-the-west-and-the-coming-age-of-global -digital-competition/.

5. See Spencer P. Boyer, "Learning from Each Other: The Integration of Immigrant and Minority Groups in the United States and Europe," Center for American Progress, April 2009, https://www.americanprogress.org/issues /security/reports/2009/04/16/5857/learning-from-each-other/.

6. Boyer, "Learning from Each Other," 6.

7. Emily Badger, "Extensive Data Shows the Punishing Reach of Racism for Black Boys," *New York Times*, March 19, 2018, https://www.nytimes.com /interactive/2018/03/19/upshot/race-class-white-and-black-men.html.

8. Antonio Flores, "How the U.S. Hispanic Population Is Changing," Pew Research Center, September 18, 2017, http://www.pewresearch.org/fact-tank /2017/09/18/how-the-u-s-hispanic-population-is-changing/.

9. U.S. Census Bureau Quick Facts: United States, 2017.

10. William H. Frey, "The U.S. Will Become 'Minority White' in 2045, Census Projects," Brookings Institution, March 14, 2018, https://www.brookings

.edu/blog/the-avenue/2018/03/14/the-us-will-become-minority-white-in
-2045-census-projects/.

11. Carroll Doherty, "5 Facts about Trump Supporters' Views of Immi-
gration," Pew Research Center, August 25, 2016; Salvador Rizzo, "Trump's
Claim That Immigrants Bring 'Tremendous Crime' Is Wrong," *Washington
Post*, January 18, 2018.

12. Boyer, "Learning from Each Other," 8.

13. Boyer, "Learning from Each Other," 8.

14. Boyer, "Learning from Each Other," 8.

15. "Migration and Migrant Population Statistics," *Eurostat Statistics
Explained*, March 2018, https://ec.europa.eu/eurostat/statistics-explained
/index.php?title=Migration_and_migrant_population_statistics#Migrant
_population:_almost_22_million_non-EU_citizens_living_in_the_EU.

16. On the decrease in asylum applications, see Stefan Lehane, "The EU
Remains Unprepared for the Next Migrant Crisis," Carnegie Europe, April
3, 2018, https://carnegieeurope.eu/2018/04/03/eu-remains-unprepared-for
-next-migration-crisis-pub-75965.

PART III

Stories as the Basis for Narrative

13

Embattled Farmers

CASS R. SUNSTEIN

A national narrative requires stories, not concepts. Here are two concepts: self-government and the equal dignity of human beings. Here are some stories.

"Fire, Fellow Soldiers, for God's Sake, Fire"

In 2017 I moved from New York to Massachusetts. My wife and I chose to live in Concord, even though we are not working there. That wasn't the most practical decision, but still, it made some sense.

Concord is breathtakingly beautiful. It is also historic. It's where the Revolutionary War started on April 19, 1775, when about seven hundred British soldiers were given what they thought were secret orders—to destroy colonial military supplies being held in Concord. That's where Paul Revere rode, where the first shots of the American Revolution were fired, where dozens of people died and dozens were badly hurt, and where our nation started to be born.

Know the phrase "the shot heard round the world"? If you'd asked me in 2016, I would have said, with complete confidence, that the it referred to Bobby Thomson's game-winning home run in 1951, which won the pennant for the Brooklyn Dodgers. Wrong answer.

The phrase is a lot older than that. Here's the start of the "Concord Hymn," written in 1836 by Concord's Ralph Waldo Emerson for the dedication of the Obelisk, a monument commemorating the Battle of Concord. You might focus on the fourth line (though I confess it is the third that really gets to me):

> By the rude bridge that arched the flood,
> Their flag to April's breeze unfurled,
> Here once the embattled farmers stood,
> And fired the shot heard round the world.

Emerson wrote that sixty-one years after the event. No single shot is known to have started the Revolutionary War, but it was in Concord that British soldiers initially confronted the American militia on Old North Bridge. The Americans were under strict orders not to shoot unless the British shot first. The British began by firing two or three shots into the Concord River; the Americans interpreted those shots as mere warnings. Consistent with their orders, they did not respond. But the British soon followed with a volley, killing two Americans, including one of their leaders, Captain Isaac Davis, who was shot in the heart—the first American officer to lose his life in the Revolution. He left a widow and five children.

Seeing this, Major John Buttrick, a leader of the Concord militia, immediately leaped up from the ground and exclaimed, "*Fire, fellow soldiers, for God's sake, fire.*" According to those who were actually there, "the word fire ran like electricity through the whole line of Americans," and "for a few seconds, the word, *fire, fire* was heard from hundreds of mouths."[1] Acting as one, Concord's embattled farmers followed Buttrick's order. Two British soldiers were killed. The rest immediately retreated. Astoundingly, the Americans won the first engagement. The American Revolution was on.

American Exceptionalism

Many people think of that particular revolution as pretty conservative, certainly as revolutions go. The French Revolution shook the world, and so did the Russian Revolution. To many people, the American Revolution seems much milder. Maybe it was a matter of escaping British rule, but without fundamental changes in people's understandings of society and politics.

After all, much of American law and culture reflects our British heritage, and in many respects, our Constitution draws directly on that heritage. Americans refer proudly to Anglo-American traditions. They love Shakespeare, Wordsworth, and the Beatles. Long before the Constitution, there was the Magna Carta. Were the British really so bad? Sure, the Americans didn't want to be ruled by a king, and no taxation without representation and all that, and we had some kind of tea party in Boston—but was there such a big break?

Yes, there was. If you study the decades that preceded the revolution, you can see the rise of republicanism everywhere, and it was a radical creed. It provides the enduring foundations of American exceptionalism.

As the American colonists saw it, republicanism entailed self-government; their objection to British rule was founded on that principle. Republicanism takes many forms, and it can be traced all the way back to Rome. But the colonists were particularly influenced by the French theorist Montesquieu, who famously divided governments into three kinds, with associated definitions, over which it is worth lingering: "A republican government is that in which the body, or only a part of the people, is possessed of the supreme power; monarchy, that in which a single person governs by fixed and established laws; a despotic government, that in which a single person directs everything by his own will and caprice."[2]

The colonies came to despise both monarchy and despotism. They thought that the former often led to the latter. If you have any doubt on that count, consider the Declaration of Independence, which objects that "a long train of abuses and usurpations" from the monarchy "evinces a design to reduce" the colonies "under absolute Despotism"—which is what led to the conclusion that "it is their right, it is their duty, to throw off such Government, and to provide new Guards for their future security."

In the colonies, republican thinking, focused on the supreme power of the body of the people, led to fresh ideas about what governments can legitimately do. More broadly, it spurred new understandings of how human beings should relate to one another and in the process undid established hierarchies of multiple kinds.

In the early 1980s, I was privileged to serve as law clerk for Justice Thurgood Marshall, one of the greatest lawyers and judges in American history and an architect of the legal strategy that struck down "separate but equal" in public schools. Marshall was also irreverent, and he had a twinkle in his eye, and he was tough. He told me a story about meeting a member of British royalty, Prince Philip, who asked him, immediately after shaking hands, "Would you like to hear my opinion of lawyers?" Marshall shot back, "Would you like to hear my opinion of princes?" Marshall's quip was an outgrowth of distinctly American thinking in the last four decades of the eighteenth century.

The best and most vivid account comes from the historian Gordon Wood, who shows that the American Revolution was social as well as political and that it involved an explosive principle: the equal dignity of human beings.[3] In the early decades of the eighteenth century, Americans lived in a traditional society that was defined by established hierarchies that affected people's daily lives, even their beliefs and their self-understandings.

Wood writes that "common people" were "made to recognize and feel their subordination to gentlemen," so that those "in lowly stations . . . developed what was called a 'down look'" and "knew their place and willingly walked while gentlefolk rode; and as yet they seldom expressed any burning desire to change places with their betters."[4] In Wood's account, it is impossible to "comprehend the distinctiveness of that premodern world until we appreciate the extent to which many ordinary people *still accepted their own lowliness*."[5] That acceptance had a political incarnation. In England, of course, national sovereignty was found in the king, and the American subjects of the king humbly accepted that understanding.

As late as 1760, the colonies consisted of fewer than two million people, subjects of the monarchy, living in economically underdeveloped communities, isolated from the rest of the world. They "still took for granted that society was and ought to be a hierarchy of ranks and degrees of dependency."[6]

Over the next twenty years, their whole world was turned upside down, as the monarchical view of the world crumbled. This was a revolution of everyday values as well as politics. In Wood's words, the American Revolution was "as radical and social as any revolution in history," producing "a new society, unlike any that had ever existed anywhere in the world."[7]

It was republicanism, with its proud commitment to liberty and equality, that obliterated the premodern world. To be sure, the transformative power of republicanism could be felt everywhere, including in England itself. As David Hume put it, "To talk of a king as God's vice-regent on earth or to give him any of these magnificent titles which formerly dazzled mankind, would but excite laughter in everyone."[8] But in the American colonies, the authority of republican thinking was especially pronounced. As the Revolution gathered steam, people were not laughing. Rule by the king wasn't funny. In 1776 Thomas Paine described the king as a "royal brute" and a "wretch" who had "the pretended title of Father of His People."[9]

With amazement, John Adams wrote that "Idolatry to Monarchs, and servility to Aristocratical Pride, was never so totally eradicated from so many Minds in so short a Time."[10] David Ramsay, one of the nation's first historians (himself captured by the British during the Revolution), marveled that Americans were transformed "from subjects to citizens," and that was an "immense" difference, because citizens "possess sovereignty. Subjects look up to a master, but citizens are so far equal, that none have hereditary rights superior to others."[11] Paine put it this way: "Our style and manner of thinking have undergone a revolution more extraordinary than the political revolution of a country. We see with other eyes; we hear with other ears; and think with other thoughts, than those we formerly used."[12]

The thinking behind the Revolution led to an attack on royalty and aristocracy, to be sure. If republicanism was about anything, it was about that. But the same thinking placed a new focus on the aspirations, the needs, and the authority of ordinary people. Hierarchies of all kinds were bound to disintegrate—not through anything like envy but through the simple assertion, immortalized in the Declaration of Independence, that all men are created equal. As Wood puts it, "To focus, as we are today apt to do, on what the Revolution did not accomplish—highlighting and lamenting its failure to abolish slavery and change fundamentally the lot of women—is to miss the great significance of what it did accomplish: indeed, the Revolution made possible the antislavery and women's rights movements of the nineteenth century and in fact all our current egalitarian thinking."[13]

In the nineteenth century, Walt Whitman, America's poet laureate, spoke for the Revolution when he wrote, "Of Equality—as if it harm'd me, giving others the same chances and rights as myself—as if it were not indispensable to my own rights that others possess the same."[14]

The Core

It's an old story, and it's probably even true. When the authors of the new American Constitution declared, after their months of work in Philadelphia, that they had finally reached consensus, one Mrs. Powel shouted a question to the revered Benjamin Franklin, then eighty-one years old: "Dr. Franklin, what have you given us, a monarchy or a republic?" He gave this answer: "A republic, if you can keep it."[15]

With those words, Franklin deflected the thrust of the question. True, he didn't refuse to answer: "A republic," he said, and not a monarchy. But in his view, the question wasn't what the framers, a band of good and great men, had given to the American people. The Constitution is not a gift. The question was what "We the People" would do with the framework that the framers had produced.

Here, I suggest, is the core of a national narrative that should unite all Americans, whatever their age, region, sex, race, religion, or political orientation. The narrative began in the colonies in the middle of the eighteenth century. Its initially defining day was April 19, 1775. The day was followed in short order by the Declaration of Independence, the Articles of Confederation, and the Constitution, with those opening words, harking back to the republican revolution: We the People.

The founding period was complemented by the Civil War and its amendments, which can be seen to have carried forward the revolutionary ideals. The movement for woman suffrage did the same. With its insistence on equal opportunity and its attack on entrenched privilege, the New Deal maintained continuity with those ideals.

The same is true of World War II, with Franklin Delano Roosevelt's words establishing continuity with Jefferson's Declaration:

> Nazi forces are not seeking mere modifications in colonial maps or in minor European boundaries. They openly seek the destruction of all elective systems of government on every continent— including our own; they seek to establish systems of government based on the regimentation of all human beings by a handful of individual rulers who have seized power by force.
>
> These men and their hypnotized followers call this a new order. It is not new. It is not order. For order among nations presupposes something enduring—some system of justice under which individuals, over a long period of time, are willing to live. Humanity will never permanently accept a system imposed by conquest and based on slavery.[16]

The Cold War, fought against the Soviet Union and Communism, was founded on the same principles. Ronald Reagan, who helped win that particular war, was right to call out "the evil empire." In doing so, he made common cause with the American revolutionaries. His emphasis was on self-government and the equal dignity of human beings.

Of course, we can disagree about what those ideals entail. We can favor a relatively strong national government or a much weaker one. We can believe in free markets, or we can believe that they must be regulated. We can like or dislike the minimum wage. We can fear climate change, or not. We can vigorously support political candidates whom our fellow citizens abhor. But we can agree that the idea of self-government rules out a lot of things and that if we are committed to human dignity, some practices are beyond the pale.

Interpretation

There is, of course, a question in the background here: How ought we to choose a national narrative?

If we are in search of such a narrative, we could tell countless tales. We could tell a tale of class and of enduring conflicts between rich and poor. We could highlight the question of race, focusing on slavery and segregation, and their legacy and regard the national experiment as irremediably flawed. We could speak of free markets and private property—their rise and their fall. We could speak of capitalism and imperialism. We could find American exceptionalism, and an accompanying national narrative, in the absence of anything like a feudal legacy and hence the failure of socialism's appeal.

To choose among competing narratives, it is useful to consult Ronald Dworkin's distinctive understanding of interpretation.[17] In Dworkin's view, interpreters have an obligation of fidelity to the existing materials, and also a duty to put them in the best constructive light. He applies the label of "integrity" to that conception of interpretation. In that view, interpreters cannot simply ignore the materials that they are charged with interpreting. They cannot just make up their own understanding. But those materials might leave them with some room to maneuver. If so, they should choose the approach that makes the most appealing account. Consider the task of someone charged with writing the next chapter in a chain novel. Authors cannot disregard the existing materials. But they might be able to turn the story in multiple directions. If so, they might ask: *What new chapter makes the story best?*

We can see the power of Dworkin's approach in judicial efforts to understand the meaning of constitutional provisions governing freedom of speech, due process of law, and equal protection. That approach also helps to explain what judges disagree about. Sometimes they disagree about the existing materials and what it means to maintain faith with them. Sometimes they disagree about what approach puts those materials in the best possible light.

The same is true with efforts to produce a national narrative. Some candidates must be rejected because they do not fit the facts; consider narratives about the triumph of fascism or theocracy. Some narratives should be rejected if only because they are unacceptably bleak, a kind of raising of the middle finger; consider efforts to understand the nation's history principally in terms of sexism or racism. Some candidates will not seem appealing, at least to too many of us; consider narratives about the nation's march to social democracy.

Here is my conclusion and my plea: an emphasis on what happened before and after the firing of shots in Concord and the courageous response of the embattled farmers maintains continuity with the historical facts and offers us something on which we can build.

Notes

1. Ezra Ripley, *With Other Citizens of Concord, a History of the Fight at Concord, on the 19th of April, 1775*, 2nd ed. (Concord: Herman Atwill, 1832).

2. Charles de Secondat, Baron de Montesquieu, *The Spirit of Laws* (London: George Bell and Sons, 1906), 8.

3. See Gordon Wood, *The Radicalism of the American Revolution* (New York: Vintage Books, 1991).

4. Wood, *The Radicalism*, 29.

5. Wood, *The Radicalism*, 29–30.

6. Wood, *The Radicalism*, 6.

7. Wood, *The Radicalism*, 6.

8. David Hume, "Whether the British Government Inclines More to Absolute Monarchy, or to a Republic," in *Complete Works of David Hume* (Hastings UK: Delphi Classics, 2016).

9. Wood, *The Radicalism of the American Revolution*, 168.

10. Hume, "Whether the British Government," 169.

11. Hume, "Whether the British Government," 169.

12. Quoted in Gordon Wood, *The Creation of the American Republic, 1776–1787*, rev. ed. (Chapel Hill: University of North Carolina Press, 1998), 48.

13. Wood, *The Radicalism*, 169.

14. Walt Whitman, "Leaves of Grass," in *The Complete Poems*, ed. Francis Murphy (New York: Penguin, 1996), 303.

15. The tale has many versions. I'm telling my favorite.

16. Franklin Delano Roosevelt, "On U.S. Involvement in the War in Europe," speech before White House Correspondents' Association, Washington DC, March 15, 1941.

17. See Ronald Dworkin, *Law's Empire* (Cambridge MA: Belknap Press of Harvard University Press, 1986).

14

America as a Social Movement

ELEANOR CLIFT

When I was thirteen years old I won an essay contest, "What the United Nations Means to Me," with Eleanor Roosevelt serving as a judge. She noted the similarity in our names. I was Eleanor Roeloffs, and getting singled out in that way by a former First Lady lauded for her human rights work made a big impression on me. I didn't know much about politics then, but I knew enough to understand that she was a driving force behind what the United Nations stood for and that I wanted to be on her side.

I learned to define my politics and values by identifying heroes to look up to and follow. I think a country does the same thing. The people we choose to elevate and remember over time signify the American narrative. In my own life, the social justice movements that shaped me individually and America as a country, which despite our problems remains the envy of the world, are the civil rights movement, the fight for women's liberation, and the mobilization against the Vietnam War.

These social movements are America's story, and they're my story as a woman born in the middle of the last century whose life was made measurably better amid these broad strokes of history.

Young people coming of age today are shaped by Black Lives Matter, the Me Too and Time's Up movements, and the advocacy for LGBTQ rights, which led to the Supreme Court legalizing same-sex marriage in a landmark ruling on June 26, 2015. The progress in this area has been remarkably swift in sweeping away political opposition once thought intractable.

For those who despair about our current state of extreme partisanship, I would urge them to turn away from partisan politics and celebrate the progress of the disability rights movement as an analogue of the gay rights and civil rights movements in freeing people to be fully productive citizens. I am also watching with enormous pride the emergence of the next generation of activists, born out of horror at mass shootings and determined to assert their right to be safe from military-style weapons.

Set in motion by Parkland, Florida, high school students who survived a school shooting that killed seventeen of their classmates, people of all ages rallied on March 24, 2018 in Washington and cities all over the country, and indeed the world, in solidarity against a permissive gun culture that sanctions military-grade weaponry in the hands of civilians claiming the protection of the Second Amendment.

Social movements take a long time. They don't make change overnight. If you ask people who waited sometimes for decades to marry the person they love whether the Supreme Court ruling in 2015 legalizing same-sex marriage happened quickly, they would likely say no, it was a long time coming. They're right, of course, but when we consider how fast things moved once the groundwork was laid, and the courts got involved, and constitutional protections were put in place, it's possible the same shift in thinking could happen around gun safety and commonsense gun laws.

A *Washington Post* / Kaiser Family Foundation poll conducted between January 24 and February 22, 2018 found that one in five Americans participated in a political rally in the previous two years, the largest mobilization since the Vietnam War. Of that group, 19 percent had never before joined in any kind of political activism. This is the kind of political engagement that can change America.

My story begins with growing up in Queens, New York, where I rarely encountered a black person and where my public school classrooms stayed almost all white despite the Supreme Court's 1954 decision in *Brown v. Board of Education* to end segregation. As a young adult in the sixties, I watched with horror the scenes on television of Bull Connor, the elected commissioner of public safety, unleashing attack dogs and turning fire hoses on black protestors in Birmingham, Alabama.

The Democratic governor of Alabama, George Wallace, stood in the schoolhouse door at the University of Alabama in June 1963, attempting to block two black students from entering. He wanted to uphold his inaugural pledge, "Segregation now, segregation tomorrow, segregation forever." Faced with National Guard troops ordered by President Kennedy to escort the students, Wallace backed down, and the whole sorry scene was captured on national television.

We didn't see anything like that in the North, so I thought the South must be a terrible place. When my first husband, who was in the advertising business, was transferred to Atlanta to work on the Delta Airlines account in 1966, I thought I was being banished to the ends of the earth. Instead, I found a city with five historically black colleges and a black middle class, which I had never seen growing up in New York. I made friends across the racial divide. A popular lunch spot for black and white to gather was the Hungry Club, located in the Butler Street YMCA in downtown Little Five Points. I lived and breathed the civil rights movement in a way that became very personal. These were people I knew and admired. When Martin Luther King Jr. was assassinated on April 4, 1968, the woman who drove him to the airport on that fateful final trip to Memphis was Xernona Clayton, a friend of the King family and someone I knew well enough to call and commiserate with and to rely upon for information well before I officially became a reporter.

I had started working for *Newsweek* in New York as secretary to the National Affairs editor, and when we moved to Atlanta, I joined the Atlanta bureau as its "girl Friday," a term that is now obsolete; that job would now be called "office manager." It's where I learned to be a reporter, quite fortuitously, as it turned out. When the women's movement took hold in the 1970s, the women in New York who were organizing a class-action suit against the magazine for gender discrimination told me to stop doing reporting, because I was being exploited.

That didn't make a lot of sense to me. If I stopped reporting, I would be relegating myself to the more narrow secretarial job. I had a wonderful boss, Joe Cumming, who was known at *Newsweek* as "the poet bureau chief" because of his love of language and his lyrical nature. He thought I was amazing because I could balance the office checkbook, and I thought he was amazing because of his literary sensibility and his generous spirit.

He would close the bureau on Wednesday afternoons so we could go to the Atlanta Library to watch the screening of Alistair Cooke's *Civilization* series. Joe said that to be a good reporter you needed to know about history. He helped me fill in the gaps in my college education. I had dropped out after a year at Hofstra College in Hempstead, New York. I also attended Hunter College in New York City for a couple of years but never got a degree. Funny, nobody seemed to care about that or even notice. It's different today, when a college degree is used to weed people out, and not getting a degree is a whole lot riskier than it was when I didn't think twice about what I might be giving up.

In my day, women gained access to the workplace by going in the side door, often in a clerical position, and proving themselves. Today, everybody goes in the front door, which is a good thing, but it's crowded. A degree is the ticket of admission.

When I first moved to Atlanta in February 1966 I was surprised to find that just about everyone still supported the Vietnam War. In New York I didn't know anyone who supported the war. As the next few years unfolded in the fateful march to 1968, the worst year ever, with the assassinations of Dr. King and Bobby Kennedy, one by one the pillars of the Atlanta Establishment peeled away from the war.

Gene Patterson, crusading editor of the *Atlanta Constitution*, stood ramrod straight before the august Commerce Club to declare his opposition to the war. He was a decorated veteran who had intended to make the military his career. Coming out against the war went against everything he thought he stood for. But his friend and mentor, pioneering civil rights journalist Ralph McGill, a proud Marine, whom Gene had succeeded as editor, had made the turn away from the war in a column that ran on the front page, so it was time.

When Dr. King was killed, *Newsweek* in New York sent gas masks to the Atlanta bureau, anticipating violence. I was very proud of my adopted city when things remained calm and the progressive white mayor, Ivan Allen Jr., riding in a police car, led a march of nearly four thousand black students through the city's neighborhoods. In the tense days between King's death and his funeral, Allen visited every black neighborhood and walked the streets to reassure the city's black residents that they had an advocate in City Hall.

Atlanta's slogan was "The City Too Busy to Hate," and while progress was far from perfect, to my eyes as a transplant from Queens, New York, the battle lines couldn't have been clearer. There was truth and justice on one side and the Klan and racism on the other. First elected mayor in 1961, Allen had defeated Lester Maddox, an avowed segregationist and populist Democrat who five years later was elected governor.

"I wasn't so all-fired liberal when I first moved into City Hall," Allen later wrote. "But when I saw what the race-baiters were doing or could do to hold back the orderly growth of Atlanta, it infuriated me and eventually swung me to the extreme end opposite them."[1]

The ten years I spent in Atlanta were a transformative time in my life. Two of my three sons were born there, and it's where I became a reporter, a career I never imagined I would have. The women's movement was beckoning, and life choices that seemed out of reach suddenly seemed possible.

The women at *Newsweek* in New York had won significant concessions. Among them, women working at the magazine were given a chance to try out as reporters or writers. I remember asking my bureau chief, Joe Cumming, if I could get one of those tryouts, and he said, sure, as long as I got someone to fill in for me at the front desk to answer the phone and greet people and balance that checkbook. That was easy. I recruited a young woman I trusted, and thanks to the courage of the women in New York who filed the first class-action suit in a major news organization to challenge gender discrimination, I got my chance.

I did a number of stories across the South in the seven states the Atlanta bureau covered, interviewing a variety of people, from George Wallace to country music singers Loretta Lynn and Tammy Wynette. I loved it, and when the summer was over, I became a full-fledged reporter. It was 1974, and Georgia governor Jimmy Carter was running for president. He was one of sixteen Democrats contending for the 1976 nomination, a varied field that included such luminaries as California governor Jerry Brown, Arizona representative Morris Udall (who would become the second-place finisher), and a half dozen senators, among them Birch Bayh, Henry "Scoop" Jackson, and Lloyd Bentsen.

Also in the race, making his fourth bid for president, was George Wallace, paralyzed from the waist down and in a wheelchair after an assassination attempt four years earlier. Hard to imagine that Wallace still had any vote-getting power, but when Carter defeated him in the all-important Florida primary, Carter was hailed for finally slaying the dragon within the branch of the Democratic Party that Wallace represented. Wallace carried only Mississippi, South Carolina, and his home state of Alabama, but in the popular vote count in all the primaries and caucuses, he was third behind Carter and Jerry Brown.

Reflecting on this today, after the election and reelection of Barack Obama as president and then the backlash from marginalized white rural communities that helped elect Donald Trump, I am concerned that America's original sin of slavery and its descendant, racism, may never be fully erased. The vigilance of social justice movements is needed now more than ever.

In the journalistic tradition, if you cover the candidate who wins the presidency, you go to the White House too. That's how I was named one of *Newsweek*'s two White House correspondents after the November 1976 election. I call it my Cinderella story. I was in the right place at the right time, and I benefited from the changing culture.

Women getting elevated was still something of a new thing, and Carter touched a nerve in the American psyche when just a few months into his presidency he announced he was sending his wife, Rosalynn, on a thirteen-day trip to seven Latin American and Caribbean nations. *Newsweek* went into high gear. This was real news, that a president would entrust his wife on such an extensive diplomatic mission, and it was controversial. The expectation was low that she could accomplish anything of merit in the male-dominated Latin culture, and the voters weren't all that keen on her taking on such a role. "Who elected her?" was the common refrain.

Columnist Meg Greenfield, writing in *Newsweek* on June 15, 1977, said the First Lady's only perceived qualification as a policymaker was her relationship to the president. The trip raised a fundamental question about the role of the First Lady, said Greenfield. "What we have here, in other words, is not an 'uppity woman' issue, but rather a question of the proper role in government of un-elected kin of elected officials."

I was new to the White House beat then, and when Jody Powell, President Carter's press secretary, tapped me on the shoulder in the press room and said the president wanted to see me, I thought that's how this assignment works. You get called in to meet with the president every so often. For the record, that was the first and only time in decades of having a press pass that I have been summoned to the oval office.

Carter greeted me, saying, "You've come to talk about my Eleanor," meaning he wanted to talk about Rosalynn's trip to Latin America. He knew *Newsweek* was doing a cover, and he was doing damage control. The reference to Eleanor was, of course, to Eleanor Roosevelt, who then and now is the gold standard for activist First Ladies. It was years later when I visited the First Ladies museum in Canton, Ohio, when I discovered that Rosalynn's full name was Eleanor Rosalynn Smith Carter.

Rosalynn's successful trip to Latin America shattered some of the stereotypes about First Ladies, paving the way for future First Ladies and the more assertive leadership style of Hillary Clinton.

As First Lady, Clinton confessed to channeling Eleanor Roosevelt when things got tough for her after the health care bill she championed failed to get a vote in Congress. She was uncertain of her role in the administration, and imagining conversations with ER helped her buck up, "or at least to grow skin as thick as a rhinoceros," Clinton wrote on June 10, 1996 in her syndicated column, Talking It Over, modeled after ER'S column, My Day, which she penned daily from 1935 to 1962.

I always thought that if I weren't a reporter covering Clinton that we would be friends. I admired her intelligence and her fortitude in the face of personal challenges and stinging political defeats, and I hope she finds some comfort in the fact that she has inspired more people, especially women, to get involved in politics because she lost a race she was supposed to win than if she had actually won. They say history is written by the winners, and the record hundreds of thousands of people who participated in the Women's March the day after President Trump's inauguration are winners too, and they will be writing the next chapters in the American narrative.

The women's movement popularized the phrase that the personal is political, and thanks to the internet and social media, more people have the tools to tell their stories and guide the history yet to be lived.

Note

1. Ivan Allen Jr. and Paul Hemphill, *Mayor: Notes on the Sixties* (New York: Simon and Schuster, 1971).

15

Yankee Ingenuity

GERARD N. MAGLIOCCA

S ometimes the best way to understand yourself is to look at what others think of you. Foreigners offer many keen insights on what makes the United States special. One of those insights is that Americans possess an uncommon degree of political common sense that makes up for the weakness of their political institutions. To these outsiders, we are more Benjamin Franklin than James Madison.

Perhaps the most famous foreign commentator on America was Alexis de Tocqueville, a French aristocrat who traveled around the country in the 1830s. Tocqueville wrote about his trip in *Democracy in America*, a book that is still widely read for its penetrating observations about our national culture. In the part of his book that discusses the Constitution, Tocqueville was far more impressed by the sensible political temperament of the United States than by the structure of its government. "Nothing has made me admire the good sense and the practical intelligence of the Americans," he wrote, "more than the way they avoid the innumerable difficulties deriving from their Federal Constitution." If he had "not succeeded in making the reader feel the importance I attach to the practical experience of the Americans, to their habits, opinions, and, in a word, their mores, I have failed in the main object of my work."[1]

An equally perceptive foreign commentator on American politics was Walter Bagehot, an English journalist who was the founding editor of the *Economist* magazine. Bagehot wrote a classic study called *The English Constitution* shortly after the end of our

Civil War in which he argued that England's unwritten constitution was superior to our written one. In Bagehot's view, the United States was a successful democracy in spite of its Constitution. "Americans now extol their institutions," Bagehot wrote, "and so defraud themselves of their due praise. . . . If they had not a genius for politics, if they had not a moderation in action singularly curious where superficial speech is so violent . . . the multiplicity of authorities in the American Constitution would long ago have brought it to a bad end. Sensible shareholders, I have heard a shrewd attorney say, can work *any* deed of settlement; and so the men of Massachusetts could, I believe, work *any* constitution."[2]

James Bryce, who later served as Britain's ambassador to the United States, followed in Tocqueville's footsteps as a young man by visiting during the 1870s and 1880s and then writing an influential book called *The American Commonwealth*. Bryce pointed out that Americans constantly asked Europeans like him, "What do you think of our institutions?" Bryce's answer was that he was dubious of what he called the "tools" provided by the Constitution, but "the defects of the tools are the glory of the workman." What he meant was that "the American people have a practical aptitude for politics, a clearness of vision and capacity for self-government never equaled in any other nation." "Such a people," Bryce concluded, "can work any Constitution."[3]

To be sure, prominent international visitors also recognized that America was a land of ideals. Gunnar Myrdal, a Swedish economist who later won the Nobel Prize, came here shortly before World War II and wrote an exhaustive criticism of racial segregation called *An American Dilemma*. Myrdal was taken with what he labeled the "American Creed," which came from the Declaration of Independence and is "centered in the belief in equality and in the rights of liberty."[4] Thomas Jefferson was, of course, the spiritual father of the American Creed. As Abraham Lincoln said in the Gettysburg Address, through the Declaration "our fathers brought forth on this continent a new nation, conceived in Liberty, and dedicated to the proposition that all men are created equal."[5]

But for the practical judgment that Tocqueville, Bagehot, and Bryce prized in Americans, the inspiration was Benjamin Franklin. Franklin was not a lawyer or a theorist. His experience came from the most practical pursuits, first as a publisher, then as a scientist, and finally as a diplomat.[6] Perhaps his most famous statement is that "in this world nothing can be said to be certain, except death and taxes."[7] And Franklin's most memorable political contribution was his closing speech at the Constitutional Convention, which argued that the proposal was worth supporting in spite of its many imperfections.[8]

In this address, Franklin explained that ideals must be tempered by compromise. "I confess," he began, "that there are several parts of this constitution which I do not at present approve, but I am not sure I shall never approve them. Having lived long, I have experienced many instances of being obliged by better information or fuller consideration, to change opinions even on important subjects, which I once thought right." "The older I grow," Franklin continued, "the more apt I am to doubt my judgment, and to pay more respect to the judgment of others. Most men indeed as well as most sects in Religion, think themselves in possession of all truth, and that wherever others differ from them it is so far error." "Thus I consent," he said, "to this Constitution because I expect no better, and because I am not sure, that it is not the best. The opinions I have had of its errors, I sacrifice to the public good." Franklin closed by "expressing a wish that every member of the Convention who may still have objections to it, would with me, on this occasion doubt a little of his own infallibility—and to make manifest our unanimity, put his name to this instrument."[9]

The challenge today is that Franklin's pragmatism is sometimes practiced but rarely preached. Though foreigners may see what lies beneath the surface of political rhetoric, a national trait cannot be sustained without proud and public American defenders. Too often their praise is reserved for our ideals or for those who fight for them. While that praise is warranted, we do not lack for that sort of courage. What we need is more courage from those who sacrifice their ideals for the public good by seeking common ground with those who hold different opinions. Learned Hand, probably the greatest judge who never served on the United States Supreme Court, echoed Franklin when he said in a 1944 speech entitled "I Am an American Day" that the "spirit of liberty is the spirit which is not too sure that it is right; the spirit of liberty is the spirit which seeks to understand the minds of other men and women; the spirit of liberty is the spirit which weighs their interests alongside its own without bias."[10] This expression of doubt is not as exciting as "Give me liberty or give me death," but that does not make the call for thoughtful give-and-take uninspired.[11]

Think about the world beyond politics. Another of Tocqueville's astute comments was that in the United States people "of all ages, all stations in life, and all types of disposition, are forever forming associations" to accomplish religious, humanitarian, and community goals. He thought that volunteerism outside of government was a critical source of values for a democracy because "feelings and ideas are renewed, the heart enlarged, and the understanding developed only by the reciprocal action of men one upon another."[12] Not surprisingly, Benjamin Franklin was the pioneer of what we now call "civic society" in his adopted hometown of Philadelphia. Among his initiatives were the University of Pennsylvania, the American Philosophical Society, the city's first lending library, and its first volunteer firefighting service. As Franklin said in his proposal for the university, education should cultivate "an inclination joined with an ability to serve mankind, one's country, friends and family."[13]

In civic society, there is no hesitation about saluting the steady efforts of those who patiently listen to competing views and then forge a consensus to achieve progress. Most of these men and women from all races, religions, and ethnic backgrounds are unknown outside of their local organization or neighborhood. They do not seek acclaim. They do not insist on getting everything or nothing. Nor do they agree on the goals that should be pursued or how they should be accomplished. But they do share a love of country that Ronald Reagan once described as "quiet, but deep" and "whose voluntary gifts support church, charity, culture, art, and education."[14]

Moderation in the pursuit of justice is a virtue central to the American narrative. Foreigners who came to these shores to learn about us saw this truth. Benjamin Franklin lived that faith and used its spirit to support the Constitution. And millions of ordinary citizens do the same. These unsung heroes put their ideals into practice every day and represent the national character that politicians and voters should strive to emulate.

Notes

1. Alexis de Tocqueville, *Democracy in America* (1835; New York: Harper & Row, 1966), 150, 284.

2. Walter Bagehot, *The English Constitution*, 2nd ed. (1872; New York: Cosimo Classics, 2007), 228.

3. James Bryce, *The American Commonwealth*, 2 vols. (London: Macmillan, 1891), 1:1, 289, 290.

4. Gunnar Myrdal, *An American Dilemma: The Negro Problem and Modern Democracy* (New York: Harper & Row, 1944), 8. Myrdal's groundbreaking work was cited by the Supreme Court in its opinion declaring racial segregation in public schools unconstitutional. See Brown v. Board of Education, 347 U.S. 483, 494n11 (1954).

5. Garry Wills, *Lincoln at Gettysburg: The Words That Remade America* (New York: Simon & Schuster, 1992), 263.

6. See generally Walter Isaacson, *Benjamin Franklin: An American Life* (New York: Simon & Schuster, 2003).

7. Benjamin Franklin to Jean Baptiste Le Roy, November 13, 1789, in *10 Works of Benjamin Franklin* (New York: Macmillan, 1907), 69.

8. The authoritative text of Franklin's address comes from Madison's notes on the Constitutional Convention. See Max Farrand, ed., *The Records of the Federal Convention of 1787* (1911; New Haven CT: Yale University Press, 1966), 2:641–43.

9. Farrand, *The Records*, 2:642, 643.

10. Gerald Gunther, *Learned Hand: The Man and the Judge*, 2nd ed. (New York: Oxford University Press, 2011), 470.

11. This quote is widely attributed to Patrick Henry. See Jean Edward Smith, *John Marshall: Definer of a Nation* (New York: Henry Holt and Company, 1996), 43.

12. Tocqueville, *Democracy in America*, 485, 487.

13. See Isaacson, *Benjamin Franklin*, 102–5, 122–23, 146–48, quote at 147.

14. Ronald Reagan, first inaugural address, January 20, 1981, Ronald Reagan Presidential Library website, www.reaganlibrary.gov.

PART IV

Skeptical Approaches to an American Story

16

American Minimalism

Why No Robust Account of National Identity
Is Possible—or Desirable

RICHARD A. EPSTEIN

Aim Lower, Achieve More

T he challenge posed to the contributors in this volume is
to find a way, any way, perhaps, to patch up the frayed
fabric of Americans' shared national identity. The task
is said to be critical, because the inability to meet the "arduous
task of weaving a new national narrative in which all Americans can see themselves" could leave the nation vulnerable and
adrift in perilous times.[1] But can this be done? Not in my view,
unless we engage in what I call American minimalism—a conscious reduction of the set of issues that we think are truly best
handled as a nation and not better addressed by smaller subnational groups: states, local governments, and, most importantly,
all sorts of smaller private organizations that are free to choose
as they please in setting their own membership and mission.

In taking this position, I do not mean to detract from the
ever more common pleas for public discourse marked by civility, restraint, and mutual respect among people with large, even
unbridgeable differences. But the psychological dimensions of
the problem should not lead us to overlook the material conditions that have stoked disagreements in recent years. Some
of those conditions, like the rise of social media, are decidedly
mixed blessings. They allow for the mobilization of public opinion, but they also allow "activists"—a word that I use with some
dread—to magnify their abusive behavior against remote targets that have no obvious means of self-defense. In this instance,

however, I shall focus my attention on a major change in substantive social policy that contributes to this difficulty.

There are two ways to think about the use of state power to alter private relations. As a classical liberal, I certainly support the use of taxation and eminent domain to overcome coordination problems that can block Pareto-efficient moves, that is, moves that leave everyone better off under the new state of affairs than under the old ones. Indeed, with government-enforced changes, the common requirement of pro rata benefits helps stabilize matters even further because it ensures that these gains are shared all around. The unique distribution of benefits thus removes the element of political contestation, which in turn should help reduce social tensions. On the other hand, today's major justification for government action is redistribution from some groups that lose to other groups that gain. These programs have two serious problems. First, they tend to be negative-sum games, whereby the losses to the losers are greater than the gains on the other side, if only because all transfer systems dull incentives for production and consume administrative and political resources. It is not that the optimal society has zero levels of redistribution; rather, as the scope of redistribution increases, the social losses and private resentments are likely to increase as well. This is exactly what has happened as the level of public expenditures on matters like defense and infrastructure (which are often badly executed as it is) has declined while transfer payments have risen.

My simple point is that the nature of public discourse does not take place in a vacuum but is heavily dependent on widely shared norms that determine which topics are proper for collective decisions and which are not. The simple thesis is that the more weight we attach to redistributive policies in the public regime, the more likely it is that the discourse will degenerate. The outcome is due to the confluence of two forces. First, the set of demands on national institutions has become greater today than ever before. But second, the political constitution (small c) is congenitally unable to satisfy the multiple demands put on our national institutions. Today the United States is home to over 325 million people who come from diverse backgrounds and who hold widely divergent views on just about every imaginable issue of politics and power, both domestic and foreign. Increased levels of polarization are evident as restless Democrats move farther to the left in search of social justice, while angry Republicans move farther to the right in order to shake off what they see as massive intrusions into their lives by government officials with whom they have nothing in common. The middle is emptying out. Across this nation, we are long past the point where the various groups are capable of persuading those who disagree with them. Indeed, too often, earnest attempts to forge a common national identity only reveal the enormous gaps in views on any issue worth talking about, often exacerbating the problem.

The only way to obtain anything like a national consensus is to pare down the public space so that individuals who disagree strongly with each other can go their separate ways or at least avoid direct confrontation. And the only way for that to happen is to reclaim the small (but not zero) government philosophy. Thus, the primary function of the state should be to supply standard, nonexcludable, public goods on such key issues as national defense, infrastructure, and the legal protection against force, fraud, and monopoly—all issues on which citizens could agree to concentrate their collective national energies. Other issues should be dealt with through voluntary organizations that recruit and maintain their own ranks. But that is not likely to happen today—multiple movements led by cadres of political activists render this "live-and-let-live" philosophy a distant echo in modern deliberations.

Everyone has a grievance against someone else, and too many groups now think these issues should be rectified through collective-action mechanisms that transfer wealth or opportunities from one group to another. The main task of government is now to address yawning inequalities of wealth, which can only be done by pitting the rich against the poor and, as a result, widening ideological gaps. Or the task is to end all imbalances associated with differences in race, gender, sexual orientation, and disability. Armed with these lofty goals, some groups think that they are entitled to invoke the coercive power of the state to regulate, tax, or criminalize the conduct of their rivals, which once again only aggravates the existing conflicts. In modern times, any offense taken at the supposed sins of others becomes a legitimate grievance for which rectification by government coercion should always be on the table, often as the preferred option.

It won't work. So long as insistent claims for rectification and redistribution dominate American public life, any hope of forging a national identity becomes ever weaker. Public life will remain in turmoil so long as national elites believe there is no escape from political and ideological confrontation with their enemies in the public space. Too few people today believe that the proper strategy for national identity is American minimalism, that is, to shrink the role of government so that it concentrates on those collective decisions necessary to the few issues of national life and death. The more every matter of daily social interaction becomes a matter of public interest and concern, the bleaker the prospect of forging any kind of national unity. Identity politics thus works against any effort to form a stable sense of national identity that can command national respect.

The Civil Rights Movement

To illustrate how these issues play out, I shall concentrate my attention here on one deep-seated source of social division today: how the civil rights movement should respond to the challenge of discrimination for or against various groups. The laws surrounding discrimination are often regarded as sacrosanct, but they need a serious reappraisal. Antidiscrimination law is a growth industry, as measured by the number of grounds on which it is now illegal to discriminate against certain individuals. These include the original grounds that were put into the Civil Rights Act of 1964 (CRA), which made it illegal for an employer "to fail or refuse to hire or to discharge any individual, or otherwise to discriminate against any individual with respect to his compensation, terms, conditions, or privileges of employment, because of such individual's race, color, religion, sex, or national origin."[2]

In essence, the CRA announced the grounds that the nation collectively thought should be irrelevant for private dealings with respect to employment. The antidiscrimination laws represent a collective judgment as to how private firms should manage their own workforces.

Since that time the list of forbidden grounds of discrimination has increased so that it now also includes, at a minimum, age, sexual orientation, and disability status. And proposals are also lurking to include more items on the list, such as obesity. The early civil rights laws were intended to flatten the ground of relevant characteristics that could be taken into account in moving toward the ideal, for as Martin Luther King Jr. stated in his famous "I Have a Dream" speech of August 28, 1963: "I have a dream that my four children will one day live in a nation where they will not be judged by the color of their skin but by the content of their character."[3] In such a society, it should be easier to deal with collective decisions concerning national identity because each person could come to the dialogue as though he or she was a representative of the whole. In more philosophical terms, King's remarks ask all individuals to address questions of national policy as if they stood behind a Rawlsian veil of ignorance, following the Kantian categorical imperative, such that they necessarily have to think about the welfare of all, and thus the national identity, in order to choose the most preferable set of outcomes for both themselves and others.

Ideally, people in this state of affairs understand that every collective decision generates its share of winners and losers, but since they have willed themselves into thinking at a higher level of abstraction and national identity, they will no longer think of themselves as members of their particular group or clan. When this process is followed universally, people will be able to rise above their own particular position on matters of political deliberation and thus engage in a form of "civic republicanism" in search of public virtue. So liberated, people speak as representatives of their better selves, free of the self-interested demands that guide them in their day-to-day set of market transactions devoted to work, education, family, and health care—all of which, and more, have become hot-button issues since that luminous day in late August 1963.

Nonetheless, none of this came to pass, and in retrospect, it could not have come to pass. Identity politics has proved too strong. The political climate in the United States in 1963 was one of transition. It is clear from reading the King speech that his major ideal was not some grand vision of social equality or national identity. Rather, it was ending the scourge of segregation that had enveloped so much of the country, South and North, since the end of the Civil War. It was for that reason that the speech contained four references to Mississippi, three to Georgia, two to Alabama, and one to Louisiana, as well as one to New York, to remind his audience that no part of the nation was exempt from his gaze. Removing these barriers to social integration is fully required by any theory of limited government under which all citizens have equal rights. Nonetheless, much more was at work here. As was common with King, his lofty aspirations were punctuated with not-so-veiled threats: "There will be neither rest nor tranquility in America until the Negro is granted his citizenship rights. The whirlwinds of revolt will continue to shake the foundations of our nation until the bright day of justice emerges."[4]

It is important to note the delicate balance in this speech. The March on Washington was officially billed as "The March on Washington for Jobs and Freedom."[5] Conceptually, these two elements—jobs and freedom—could not be more antithetical to each other. Freedom implies that all citizens, regardless of race, have the equal right to deal with each other in a competitive market, free of the shackles of government regulations that favor some over others. The traditional rule is that all transactions are at will, so that people can refuse to cooperate with others for a good reason, a bad reason, or no reason at all. The protection for parties on both sides of the market is the abundance of choices on the other side of the market. There is no right to force any unwilling party to enter into transactions by restricting the grounds on which they decline to do business.

This common-law rule has an exception: it does not apply to

those industries like public utilities and common carriers that enjoy a legal or natural monopoly: they do have the obligation to serve the public at reasonable and nondiscriminatory rates. But lest there be any confusion about the matter, the term "nondiscriminatory" is used here in an antiredistributive sense. It is intended to make sure that no group of customers gains a cross-subsidy from any other group, so that high-risk customers pay more than those who are low-risk. Discrimination in this context does not mean that all customers receive the same rates regardless of race, sex, or age; that system would introduce major cross-subsidies and become the source of divisive contestation, as with the nondiscriminatory rates imposed under the Affordable Care Act.

Jobs are an entirely different proposition. In the modern context, activists desire not merely that people have a right to take the job offers that come their way; instead, the state is duty-bound to supply them jobs on a set of favorable terms that are, to put it mildly, difficult to determine. But King's vision was the proper path; one reason why his March on Washington speech had universal appeal is that it referred to freedom nineteen times and to jobs not even once. And while it called for the end of segregation, it called neither for reparations nor for income equality. King's targets may seem modest today, but they were critical in their own time. Most importantly, they were not divisive but could form one building block in the quest for a national identity that rested, at least in part, on the principle of equal opportunity for all under law, regardless of race, creed, or sex.

In retrospect, however, King's vision of equal opportunity was only a passing phase in the civil rights movement. The March on Washington speech preceded the great social unrest that erupted into violence in many key cities: Baltimore, Chicago, Detroit, Los Angeles, Newark, and New York. The rioting started before the assassination of King in Nashville in 1968, and it intensified thereafter. The great achievement of the March on Washington was that it led, after the assassination of John F. Kennedy in November 1963, to the passage of the color-blind Civil Rights Act of 1964, which took great pains to block any preferential treatment (later known as affirmative action) that was designed to redress wrongs that occurred prior to the passage of the act, especially in connection with discrimination by labor unions. But at this point the social consensus on the proper public response to race diverges: some individuals continued to harbor the earlier vision that the past inequities would be erased by time, while others said that a color-blind regime could not respond to the unique stresses and demands of the time. For example, waiting for an often-dysfunctional educational system to right itself could take at least a generation. Worse still, there were many strong forces, chiefly unions, that were prepared to block the innovations— such as vouchers and charter schools—that could have a stronger positive impact on educational achievement in the short run.

During this period, however, virtually no one was prepared to take the position (as I came to believe in the early 1980s) that the entire civil rights law governing private employment in competitive markets was a mistake, precisely because it empowered the Congress, the president, the Equal Opportunity Employment Commission, and the courts to make collective decisions on how the program of racial amelioration would proceed.[6] So, during this period, the process of dealing with past discrimination became far more divisive, especially in union settings. It became all too clear after *United Steelworkers of America v. Weber* that the only way in which preferential treatment could be given to black citizens was for the government to disadvantage certain white citizens, who were excluded solely on account of their race.[7] Because the practical regime left in place previous decisions that gave certain white workers their positions of high seniority, a typical feature of union collective bargaining agreements, the process of affirmative action began with new hires, typically, young individuals who were neither the architects nor the beneficiaries of the earlier discriminatory regimes.

While making these decisions business by business is a ticklish process, the absence of a single national policy actually helps ease the tensions. If firms are permitted—but not required—to employ affirmative action, individuals aggrieved with one employer's affirmative action decisions need not face an industry-wide phalanx. Private employers, moreover, must internalize a large fraction of both the benefits and costs of these difficult decisions, so that they have every incentive to fine-tune their responses by making adjustments as they learn what works and what does not for their particular firm in their particular situation. By contrast, government diktats of national policy are imposed by public officials who, while fully invested in the civil rights movement, bear none of the adverse consequences of their decisions on private firms for whom racial hiring policies are only one portion of the policy mix. Entrusting these choices to the government raises the political heat but does little if anything to inform or, rightly, reform the situation. It did not help that the opponents of affirmative action also sought a collective solution, namely, to insist on a color-blind policy that is at variance with the sentiment of most Americans. National identity does not hold when one political bloc wants to *ban* the same practice that its rivals want to require. Letting all groups go their own way is far wiser.

The situation has only become more difficult by the expansion of the protected groups under the various civil rights laws. In the decades following 1964, the new claim was not for equal treatment under law but rather for an equal share of social resources—the difference between equality of opportunity and equality of result. For instance, it makes no sense to claim that disabled individuals must have access to jobs or facilities that are not suited for their needs. But given their talent, some employers will choose to specialize in hiring such workers, at least if they are able to make investments in facilities that can be amortized over a sufficiently large number of workers that need the same form of assistance. In this regard, technological improvements can do far more than government commands to ease the strains. There is no need to place the question in the public domain when solutions can be found in decentralized decision making.

Nonetheless, the current law spurns private solutions by individual firms because they move too slowly. One possible way to increase the rate of change would be to offer government subsidies to make certain places suitable for various classes of workers. Such a program could easily degenerate into rent seeking and generate inefficiency, but those defects are far smaller than those associated with the test for discrimination set out by the Americans with Disabilities Act, which imposes a collective requirement that all employers, regardless of their specific position, make "reasonable accommodations," legally determined, for workers. The objection here is not to the abstract ideal of accommodating those with disabilities; many businesses would make these accommodations anyhow. Instead, my objection runs toward any state program in which politically motivated government actors have to oversee marginal adjustments by private firms when their knowledge base is always remote and otherwise insufficient to the task. These costs are not trivial—indeed, in new construction these mandates can easily increase project costs by ten to twenty without taking into account the implicit costs of having to operate in what can be an inferior facility. Those funds could easily have been spent on other activities that, in different ways perhaps, could also be useful for society at large. But once the new system is put into place it becomes perfectly clear that the antidiscrimination laws pave the way for massive cross-subsidies that breed intense political competition, reinforcing the identity politics that hampers the emergence of any cautiously framed national identity.

A similar story can be told with age discrimination statutes, which offer extensive protection to older persons who generally have more financial wherewithal and professional options. The result is usually a cross-subsidy from the young to the old. A particularly telling example is in universities with tenured faculty. That system of tenure only worked before the adoption of the Age Discrimination in Employment Act (ADEA) because the mandatory retirement rules adopted virtually everywhere placed an upper bound on the level of protection received by tenured faculty. But once the mandate was removed by statute the system became lopsided. No one inside universities would say publicly what they knew privately, namely, that keeping mandatory retirement rules was a good idea. The point here does not rest on any nasty stereotype that all older faculty members become unproductive as they age; rather, simply, it is undeniably true that around retirement the variance in academic ability does increase with age. Mandatory retirement essentially allows universities to reset the table. Faculty members who are still productive can obtain positions—perhaps at lower salaries, perhaps not—at other universities or elsewhere, while those who are less able to work are shielded financially by their pension programs. But once the ADEA was enacted, covered seniors could hold on to their protected positions, reducing the normal opportunities for the advancement of younger professors. This has created a generation of academic migrants who work many non-tenure-track jobs for relatively low wages. And we know that the system is inefficient, because the same universities that silently acquiesced in lifting mandatory retirement promptly went about designing programs allowing them to buy out senior faculty members for hefty sums (usually approaching two years' salary) in order to free up space to hire younger faculty. What started out as a program intended to secure a form of justice turns out to be yet another transfer program, introducing yet another source of inefficiency and discord into the system.

More explosive still is the relentless insistence on proportionate representation of women and minority persons in education, business, and government. The operative phrase everywhere is "diversity and inclusion." Much of this movement is privately driven, but it would be a mistake to ignore the enormous level of government pressure on this front, stemming in part from the aggressive enforcement of the antidiscrimination laws in employment and in education, symbolized by the "Dear Colleague Letter" sent out in 2011 by the Office of Civil Rights in the Obama administration.[8] In universities the movement has led to the adoption of a two-tier system of preferential treatment that has resulted in relative radicalization, given that in the humanities and social sciences the overwhelming proportion of new faculty hires in recent years has come from the far-left side of the political spectrum, roughly correlating to the contemporaneous movement leftward of the Democratic Party. One simple measure of this is the percentage of contributions by faculty to Democratic and Republican candidates. Consider that in the 2012 presidential campaign (featuring Mitt Romney, not Donald Trump) the Ivy League's percentage of Democratic support ranged from a high of 97 percent at Yale to a low of 78 percent at Dartmouth, reflecting a huge degree of polarization born of a confluence of external pressures and internal preferences that was strengthened with each new hiring cycle.[9] There is no question that these trends would be powerful even if government did not put its enforcement thumb on the scale. But there is also no question that organized and aggressive civil rights enforcement at the national, state, and local levels has intensified the trend, and with it the divisive politics that drive national elections as excluded groups exact a certain measure of revenge at the polls.

The elite universities are populated with cadres of students that make their way into the professional, business, and academic elites. The consequence is a reinforcement of geographical separation to match economic segregation. The major large cities are increasingly an ever darker blue, while the rest of the country is an ever darker red—which in 2016 led to the election of Donald Trump as president in what should be regarded as a protest by the "deplorables," who turned that epithet into a badge of honor.

Prospects for the Future

What, then, are the prospects for a change in the general culture? The outlook is bleak. There is no large constituency today that thinks that limited government will help solve the growing problem of social strife. Both on the left and the right, powerful forces want to take control of the reins of government and move them in their preferred direction. The trend is more powerful on the left than on the right, but it is present on both sides of the spectrum. It is sometimes said that political deliberation is the way to slow forces of destabilization, but today that is largely a false hope. The patterns of deliberation are likely to follow the patterns of social control. If interest groups know that they can benefit enormously from getting or blocking transfer payments by putting together some winning coalition, then that is precisely what they will do. They will try to rally a winning coalition and will count it as a plus if, in the process, they can alienate a large proportion of their opponents. A weak system of property rights, whereby a wide range of land use, insurance, and financial regulation can be pressed into service to achieve this end, is part of the process.

To give but one example, two of the signature achievements (so-called) of the Affordable Care Act have done much to destabilize insurance markets: first, the prohibition against insurance companies taking preexisting conditions into account, and second, the requirement that insurance in the individual market be sold under a community rating system. Both of these programs have resulted in the creation of unsustainable cross-subsidies, leading young and healthy individuals to exit the system in droves and creating an affordability and availability crisis for the brave souls that remain behind. Yet the champions of this program do not mind that the cost of caring for the elderly, many of whom have stashed away savings, falls on the younger, and poorer, portion of the population—a form of redistribution gone haywire, as the market continues to implode because private insurers cannot avoid losses while trying to serve the individual market.

Perverse results like this continue to materialize, to which the dominant response is always to search for a way to win the political struggle rather than to call it off. But no group will secure a final victory anytime soon. Therefore, so long as every policy problem is subject to national "solution" we lose the ability to focus on the few issues that necessarily require a collective response. Hence the plea for American minimalism to focus and reframe the collective national agenda on the few things critical to national survival. The odds are long indeed. It is far harder to restore a broken political system than it is to keep it in place to begin with, and the strong interest groups are not going away anytime soon. But perhaps their force can be moderated if the uncommitted public understands the dangerous threat to national identity when interest group politics and redistributive programs top everyone's political agenda. American minimalism is a tentative first step in the right direction.

Notes

1. Robert P. Jones, "The Collapse of American Identity," *New York Times*, May 2, 2017, https://www.nytimes.com/2017/05/02/opinion/the-collapse-of -american-identity.html.

2. Civil Rights Act of 1964, 42 U.S.C. § 2000e-2.

3. Martin Luther King Jr., "I Have a Dream by Martin," August 28, 1963, http://avalon.law.yale.edu/20th_century/mlk01.asp.

4. King, "I Have a Dream by Martin."

5. "March on Washington," History.com, 2009, https://www.history.com /topics/black-history/march-on-washington.

6. See Richard A. Epstein, "The Defense of the Contract at Will," *University of Chicago Law Review* 51 (1984): 947.

7. United Steelworkers of America v. Weber, 443 U.S. 193 (1979).

8. "Dear Colleague Letter," U.S. Department of Education Office for Civil Rights, April 4, 2011, https://www2.ed.gov/about/offices/list/ocr/letters /colleague-201104.html.

9. Christopher Peek, "Yale Faculty Give Big to Democrats," *Yale Daily News*, November 16, 2012, https://yaledailynews.com/blog/2012/11/16/89811/.

17

One Nation Divisible

ALAN TAYLOR

R ecently, I took a tour of Thomas Jefferson's restored home,
Monticello, near Charlottesville, Virginia. Judging from
appearances and conversation, the group included a
broad spectrum of American tourists with diverse politics. All,
however, gasped in horror when the guide noted that Jefferson
wanted every generation to rewrite its fundamental constitutions.
"What would you think about holding a new constitutional convention today?" he asked. You might as well have asked everyone
if they would welcome bodily mutilation by space aliens. Nothing could be more terrifying than inviting contemporary politicians to rework the federal Constitution. That terror derives
in part from the real flaws of leaders today, but in equal part it
reflects a mythic inflation of the Founders as uniquely prescient
and self-sacrificing. That myth unites us only in wrangling over
what they expected.

Like sausage making, the crafting of the early American republic looks best from a distance. The revolutionaries often expressed
bitter frustration with the flaws and impugned the motives of
their peers. Diverse and fractious, the colonists lacked common
bonds as Americans. Instead, they shared mutual distrust of
their new states. John Adams of Massachusetts explained: "The
Colonies had grown up under Constitutions of Government, So
different, there was so great a Variety of Religions, they were
composed of So many different Nations, their Customs, Man-
ners and Habits had So little resemblance, and their Intercourse
had been so rare and their Knowledge of each other So imper-

fect, that to unite them in the Same Principles in Theory and the Same System of Action was certainly a very difficult Enterprize." In 1777 a congressman expressed disgust at the intrigues and wrangling in the Continental Congress. He assured Jefferson: "Rely on it, our Confederacy is not founded on Brotherly Love." Only the pressures of war against the British superpower could force the Americans of different states to cooperate.[1]

Patriots wanted a confederation just strong enough to wage the war and present a reasonably united front sufficient to persuade France to make an alliance. By keeping peace among their states, they also hoped to prevent the bloody contentions for power like those that roiled Europe. During the late 1770s congressmen felt alarmed by armed conflict between New Yorkers and New Englanders in Vermont and by rival settlers and speculators from Connecticut and Pennsylvania over the Susquehanna Valley. By forming a union, the member states sought to define their boundaries and preserve authority within those bounds. Americans needed a union to manage differences and distrust.[2]

During the 1770s Patriots also meant to keep Congress too weak to interfere in the domestic policies of the member states. Fighting against Britain's centralizing power, few wanted to create a consolidated nation on this continent. While the pressures of war pushed states together, the dread of central power kept pulling them apart. The smaller states—New Jersey, Delaware, Rhode Island, and New Hampshire—especially feared domination by the larger ones, including Massachusetts, New York, and Virginia. A national collective interest seemed elusive, as every state's leaders pushed their own agendas and threatened to secede if frustrated.[3]

The revolutionaries found it easier to declare independence than form a confederation. Not until November 1777, more than a year after declaring independence, did Congress agree on Articles of Confederation. Because ratification required unanimous approval by the thirteen states, the Articles did not become effective until 1781. The member states formed "a firm league of friendship with each other, for their common defense, the security of their Liberties, and their mutual and general welfare." Under the

Articles, the states conceded only a few, limited powers to Congress: to wage war, conduct diplomacy, and arbitrate disputes between the states.[4]

The Articles built an alliance of states rather than a cohesive nation. Adams characterized Congress as a "diplomatic assembly" of ambassadors from thirteen sovereign states. Edmund Randolph of Virginia agreed: "Congress was an assemblage of different diplomatic corps, rather than a national senate." Congress was not a national legislature that could frame laws and impose them on the states or citizens. Able only to request, Congress relied on state legislatures to adopt and execute essential laws, such as those to recruit soldiers. Congress also lacked the powers, long exercised by the Crown over colonies, to regulate trade or veto state laws. "We have no coercive or legislative Authority," declared Thomas Burke of North Carolina. "Our Constituents are bound only in Honour to observe our Determinations." He added that "the states alone had Power to act coercively against their Citizens."[5]

The federal government remained poor and weak for want of the power to levy its own taxes. After the war ended in 1783, the states increasingly went their own way, defaulting on contributions, adopting their own ineffectual trade regulations, and squabbling over boundaries. The American navy vanished, and the army shrank to a few hundred men, mostly running for their lives from Indians on the frontier. France's minister to the United States dismissed the confederation as "an incomplete and irregular System of government." Spain's ambassador reported that the United States was "almost without Government, without a Treasury, or means of obtaining money, and torn between hope and fear of whether or not their Confederation can be consolidated." A North Carolina congressman agreed that "the Confederated compact is no more than a rope of sand, and if a more efficient Government is not obtained, a dissolution of the Union must take place."[6]

That prospect did not daunt Thomas Jefferson, for he expected that the end of the war would dissolve Congress, which could lapse until there was another great crisis: "The constant session of Congress cannot be necessary in time of peace, and their separation will destroy the strange idea of their being a permanent body."[7]

Other Americans were more fearful, noting the growing recriminations between northern and southern leaders and threats by western settlements to secede to form their own governments and ally with Spain or Britain for protection. Alexander Hamilton worried that the states were "little, jealous, clashing, tumultuous commonwealths, the wretched nurseries of unceasing discord." Benjamin Franklin agreed: "Our States are on the point of separation, only to meet hereafter for the purpose of cutting one another's throats."[8]

Worse still, conflicts between the states would invite manipulation, invasion, and domination by foreign empires. John Jay of New York warned that the United States could split "into three or four independent and probably discordant republics or confederacies, one inclining to Britain, another to France, and a third to Spain, and perhaps played off against each other by the three" empires in perpetual, destructive wars.[9]

During the mid-1780s, an economic depression deepened the political crisis. Debt cases clogged the courts, and the money supply fell far short of the demands to pay taxes and creditors. Unease grew as populist politicians in state legislatures called for inflationary paper money and for suspending the collection of taxes and debts until the economy improved. When legislatures balked, farmers rioted and shut down courts. In Virginia in 1787 Reverend Matthew Maury worried, "From the Distresses & the general Discontent of the People I take it for granted we are on the Eve of a Revolution."[10]

The weak Union contributed to the economic woes, for Congress lacked the power to negotiate favorable commercial treaties with European empires—particularly Britain. Led by George Washington, a Federalist movement emerged formed of politicians willing to sacrifice state sovereignty to empower an American nation with enough might to command respect overseas. Federalists also wanted a nation strong enough to rescue any state imperiled by internal rebellion. Such a Union also seemed essential to avert wars between the fractious states. A Virginia lawyer predicted, "An independent Sovereignty in each state will directly & immediately produce scenes of blood amongst ourselves, & make us an easy prey to the first powerful foreign invader."[11]

In 1787 in Philadelphia a convention of delegates drafted a new federal Constitution, which provided a stronger national government that could directly tax the people in the states, regulate interstate trade, and deal with foreign nations from a position of strength. A merchant hailed the constitution as "the salvation of America. For at present there is hardly the semblance of Law or Government in any of the States, and for want of a Superintending Power over the whole, a dissolution [of the Union] seems to be impending."[12]

The delegates crafted a useful fiction: that a united, homogeneous, and sovereign American people created the Constitution. Hence, the document begins with "We the People" rather than "We the States." In fact, in 1787 there was scant evidence that the diverse and squabbling Virginians, New Englanders, Carolinians, New Yorkers, and Pennsylvanians thought and acted as Americans. A supporter of the new constitution privately conceded, "Instead of feeling as a nation, a state is our country. We look with indifference, often with hatred, fear, and aversion to the other states." The delegates crafted the new constitution to manage distrust by their states lest they fall into bloody civil wars. Hamilton warned, "If we should be disunited, . . . our liberties would be prey to the means of defending ourselves against the ambition and jealousy of each other." Mutual suspicion forced them together in a stronger union that was, as one scholar put it, a "peace pact." For political ends, the Founders asserted the existence of an American people as an act of faith. They hoped to generate a self-fulfilling prophecy for the future. American national identity would emerge later, slowly, painfully, and partially.[13]

Ratifying the new constitution meant a hard fight in many states, where "Anti-Federalists" distrusted any consolidation of power by a nation. After escaping from the British Empire, they dreaded an American nation as a new threat to the cherished autonomy of their states. Edmund Randolph recalled, "To

mention the surrender of one atom of sovereignty, as a contribution to a continental reservoir, was to awaken a serious alarm."[14]

In June 1788 Virginia's state ratification convention met in Rich-
mond and seemed evenly split, with, as one witness put it, "Half
of the Crew hosting sail for the land of Energy—and the other
looking with a longing aspect on the Shore of Liberty." Witnesses
feared violence between the Federalists and Anti-Federalists. A
merchant reported, "You never saw your Country Men so much
agitated, not even at the time of Cornwallis's Invasion, every
Man warm for or against the measure & nothing but debate and
altercation in all companies." On June 13 ominous weather disrupted the meeting, "a very Heavy storm of Hail, wind & rain,
which blew open the Windows, & render[e]d the House too wet
& uncomfortable to proceed" for a day.[15]

The passionate oratory of the leading Anti-Federalist, Patrick
Henry, provided another storm. A worried Federalist concluded
that Henry was "better adapted to carry his point & lead the
ignorant people astray than any other person upon earth. Madison's plain, ingenious, & elegant reasoning is entirely thrown
away and lost among such men." In fact, Madison's Federalist
reasoning carried the day. On June 25 the delegates narrowly
ratified the federal Constitution, making Virginia the tenth and
largest state to do so. A diarist recorded, "The scene was truly
awful & solemn."[16]

Jefferson missed that ratification struggle, for he remained
in Paris as the American minister to France. He returned to the
United States to join the cabinet of Washington, the first president under the new constitution. In 1791 Jefferson and his friend
James Madison soured on the growing power of the secretary
of the treasury, Alexander Hamilton. Supported by Washington,
Hamilton sought to consolidate a national government with a
powerful military, a central bank, and robust tax revenues. Jefferson and Madison organized an opposition party, the Republicans, who denounced the Federalists as crypto-Loyalists bent
on subverting republicanism to erect a British-style monarchy,
with Washington as its supposed stooge. In response, Federalists derided the Republicans as Jacobins, akin to the murderous

radicals of the French Revolution, which had erupted in 1789 and become more divisive in American politics by 1794.[17]

In 1797 another Federalist, John Adams, succeeded George Washington as president. Adams and the Federalist Congress exploited American diplomatic tensions with France to prepare for war. The Federalists enlarged the army and navy, raised taxes, and adopted restrictions on immigration and dissent known as the Alien and Sedition Acts. Federalists hoped to discredit their Republican critics as treacherous supporters of French subversives. Highlighting Jefferson's unorthodox religious views, they cast him as an atheist bent on destroying Christianity.[18]

Republicans denounced the Alien and Sedition Acts as further proof that the Federalists were would-be aristocrats undermining free speech and republicanism. In November 1798 the Kentucky state legislature adopted provocative resolutions written by Jefferson, who insisted that the states had created the Union as a diplomatic compact. Therefore, any state legislature could determine the constitutionality of federal laws and nullify their execution within that state's bounds. Virginia's legislature adopted similar resolutions, drafted by Madison.[19]

In the pivotal national election of 1800, Republicans campaigned against the unpopular federal taxes and Sedition Act prosecutions. They captured both houses of Congress and elected Jefferson as president and Aaron Burr of New York as vice president. Because Jefferson and Burr finished tied in the Electoral College returns, the lame-duck Federalist Congress tried to make trouble by pushing Burr for the presidency. For a suspenseful week, the House was deadlocked while Federalists and Republicans muttered about preparing for civil war. At last, in mid-February 1801, one moderate Federalist abstained, which broke the deadlock in favor of Jefferson.[20]

The triumphant Republicans claimed to have saved America's Republican revolution from Federalist subversion. The newly elected Congress killed the Alien and Sedition Acts, rolled back federal taxes, and radically shrank the federal government, including the military. Halting the Federalist drive to build a powerful national government, the Republicans favored a decentralized

Union that entrusted to the states all responsibilities except foreign affairs, customs collection, a barebones military, and the postal service.[21]

For the next two generations, Jefferson's principles of a limited federal government and robust states' rights prevailed in the Union. But Hamilton's principles revived during the 1860s, when a new and very different Republican Party championed liberty and union as intertwined and inseparable. The new Republicans spooked the southern states into seceding from the Union as a last, desperate measure to protect slavery. Most northerners, however, fought for the Union as perpetual and supreme. Leading that defense, Abraham Lincoln had the good political sense to deploy Hamilton's principles in Jeffersonian rhetoric. Victory in the Civil War enhanced the federal government, as did subsequent world wars and the Cold War in the next century. But a sort of Jeffersonian purism persists and has grown into a roar in recent years, provoking a renewed division of the nation, expressed with an anger reminiscent of the 1780s, 1790s, and 1850s.[22]

Americans often romanticize the Founders of the nation as united and resolute in order to rebuke current politicians as lesser beings. Pundits insist that Americans could reunite by returning to an ideal vision of our republic set by the Founders. But which Founders, and what vision? Far from uniting on fundamentals, they clashed over what form the Republic should take. Should Americans follow Thomas Jefferson's vision of a decentralized country, or do we prefer Alexander Hamilton's push for a powerful, centralized nation that promotes economic development and global power? Instead of offering a single, cohesive, and enduring plan, the diverse Founders generated contradictions that continue to divide Americans.[23]

Indeed, the federal Constitution, which we now so fetishize as a source of unity, was created in response to the dangerous disunity of a fragile new aggregation of diverse and fractious states. During the 1780s those states seemed ripe for civil wars and foreign manipulation. To avert that fate, some of the Founders wrote an ambiguous constitution that made the document easier to ratify, enabling a coalition of different views to find what they wanted in it. In the longer run, however, that ambiguity has rendered our Constitution far harder to interpret, breeding disputes that continue to roil our politics. Like a kaleidoscope, every generation remakes combinations of clashing principles derived from the revolutionary generation.

There is no single unifying narrative linking past and present in America. Instead, we have enduring divisions in a nation even larger and more diverse than that of 1787. The best we can do today is to cope with our differences by seeking compromises, just as the Founders had to do, painfully and incompletely in the early Republic. Recognizing their limitations and divisions would help us deal more frankly with our own political dilemmas.

Notes

1. John Adams to Hezekiah Niles, February 13, 1818, Founders Online, National Archives, http://founders.archives.gov/documents/Adams /99–02–02–6854; John Harvie to Thomas Jefferson, October 18, 1777, in *Papers of Thomas Jefferson*, ed. Julian Boyd et al. (Charlottesville: University of Virginia Press, 1950), 2:34–36; Don Higginbotham, "War and State Formation in Revolutionary America," in *Empire and Nation: The American Revolution in the Atlantic World*, ed. Eliga H. Gould and Peter S. Onuf (Baltimore MD: Johns Hopkins University Press, 2005), 94; Gordon S. Wood, *The Creation of the American Republic, 1776–1787* (Chapel Hill: University of North Carolina Press, 1969), 354–59.

2. David C. Hendrickson, "The First Union: Nationalism versus Internationalism in the American Revolution," in Gould and Onuf, *Empire and Nation*, 40–42; Peter S. Onuf, "The Empire of Liberty: Land of the Free and Home of the Slave," in *The World of the Revolutionary American Republic: Land, Labor, and the Conflict for a Continent*, ed. Andrew Shankman (New York: Routledge, 2014), 198–99; Jack N. Rakove, *The Beginnings of National Politics: An Interpretive History of the Continental Congress* (Baltimore MD: Johns Hopkins University Press, 1979), 142–43, 156–64, 178–79; Leonard J. Sadosky, *Revolutionary Negotiations: Indians, Empires, and Diplomats in the Founding of America* (Charlottesville: University of Virginia Press, 2009), 84–85.

3. Hendrickson, "First Union," 37–39, 45; Higginbotham, "War and State Formation," 60–61, 64; Benjamin H. Irvin, *Clothed in Robes of Sovereignty: The Continental Congress and the People Out of Doors* (New York: Oxford University Press, 2011), 274–76; Rakove, *Beginnings*, 148–76; Wood, *Creation*, 357.

4. Eliga H. Gould, *Among the Powers of the Earth: The American Revolution and the Making of a New World Empire* (Cambridge MA: Harvard University Press, 2012), 10–11; Hendrickson, "First Union," 36–37; Rakove, *Beginnings*, 158–59; Wood, *Creation*, 356–57.

5. John Adams to Thomas Jefferson, March 1, 1787 ("diplomatic assembly"), Founders Online, National Archives, http://founders.archives.gov/documents /Adams/99-02-02-0072; Edmund Randolph, "Essay on the Revolutionary History of Virginia, 1774–1782," *Virginia Magazine of History and Biography* 44 (January 1936): 46–47; Hendrickson, "First Union," 37–42; Rakove, *Beginnings*, 163–92, Thomas Burke quoted on 167; Wood, *Creation*, 355–56.

6. Diego de Gardoqui quoted in *Independence Lost: Lives on the Edge of the American Revolution*, by Kathleen DuVal (New York: Random House, 2015), 334 ("almost without"); John Jay to John Adams, October 14, 1785 ("Our federal"), and Adams to Jay, October 15, and December 3, 1785, in *Documents of the Emerging Nation: U.S. Foreign Relations, 1775–1789*, ed. Mary A. Giunta, 2 vols. (Wilmington DE: Scholarly Resources, 1998), 2:863, 864–65, 940–41; Max M. Edling, *A Revolution in Favor of Government: Origins of the U.S. Constitution and the Making of the American State* (New York: Oxford University Press, 2003), 86–87; Woody Holton, *Unruly Americans and the Origins of the Constitution* (New York: Hill & Wang, 2007), 137–38, 143–44; Gould, *Among the Powers*, 127; Rakove, *Beginnings*, 163–92; Chevalier de La Luzerne quoted in Sadosky, *Revolutionary Negotiations*, 118 ("an incomplete").

7. Thomas Jefferson to Barbe-Marbois, December 5, 1783, and Jefferson to James Madison, May 8, 1784, in Boyd et al., *Papers of Thomas Jefferson*, 6:373–74, 7:232–35.

8. Benjamin Franklin quoted in *A Brilliant Solution: Inventing the American Constitution*, by Carol A. Berkin (New York: Harcourt, 2002), 164; David C. Hendrickson, "Escaping Insecurity: The American Founding and the Control of Violence," in *Between Sovereignty and Anarchy: The Politics of Violence in the American Revolutionary Era*, ed. Patrick Griffin et al. (Charlottesville: University of Virginia Press, 2015), 219–20; Alexander Hamilton quoted in *A Is for American: Letters and Other Characters in the Newly United States*, by Jill Lepore (New York: Alfred A. Knopf, 2002), 19.

9. John Jay quoted in DuVal, *Independence Lost*, 320; Peter S. Onuf, "The Expanding Union," in *Devising Liberty: Preserving and Creating Freedom in the New American Republic*, ed. David T. Konig (Stanford CA: Stanford University Press, 1995), 59–60.

10. Edmund Pendleton to James Madison, June 16, 1783, Madison to Thomas Jefferson, May 12, 1786, and Madison to James Monroe, June 4, 1786, in *Papers of James Madison*, ed. William T. Hutchinson et al., 17 vols. to date (Chicago and Charlottesville: University of Chicago Press and University of Virginia Press, 1962–), 7:81–85, 9:48–54, 73–74; John Tyler to Jefferson, May 20, 1784, Jefferson to Alexander McCaul, April 19, 1786, and Alexander Donald to Jef-

ferson, November 12, 1787, in Boyd et al., *Papers of Thomas Jefferson*, 7:277–78, 9:388–90, 12:345–48; Matthew Maury to James Maury, December 10, 1787, in *The Documentary History of the Ratification of the Constitution*, ed. John P. Kaminski et al., 10 vols. (Madison: State Historical Society of Wisconsin, 1988), 8:228.

11. Archibald Stuart to John Breckenridge, October 21, 1787, and William Fleming to Thomas Madison, February 19, 1788, in Kaminski et al., *Documentary History*, 8:89, 383 ("independent Sovereignty").

12. Alexander Donald to Thomas Jefferson, November 12, 1787, in Boyd et al., *Papers of Thomas Jefferson*, 12:345–48 ("the salvation").

13. Richard R. Beeman, *Plain, Honest Men: The Making of the American Constitution* (New York: Random House, 2009), 380–81; Terry Bouton, *Taming Democracy: "The People," the Founders, and the Troubled Ending of the American Revolution* (New York: Oxford University Press, 2007), 182; Sam Haselby, *The Origins of American Religious Nationalism* (New York: Oxford University Press, 2015), 1; Fisher Ames quoted in Merrill Jensen, "The Sovereign States: Their Antagonisms and Rivalries and Some Consequences," in *Sovereign States in an Age of Uncertainty*, ed. Ronald Hoffman and Peter J. Albert (Charlottesville: University of Virginia Press, 1981), 228 ("Instead of feeling"); Alexander Hamilton, "Federalist No. 8," November 20, 1787, in *Papers of Alexander Hamilton*, ed. Harold C. Syrett, 27 vols. (New York: Columbia University Press, 1961–87), 4:326–32 ("if we should be disunited").

14. Archibald Stuart to John Breckinridge, June 19, 1788, in Kaminski et al., *Documentary History*, 10:1651; Randolph, "Essay," 110.

15. James Duncanson to James Maury, June 7, 1788, Theodorick Bland to Arthur Lee, June 13, 1788, and diary of William Heth, June 13, 1788, in Kaminski et al., *Documentary History*, 10:1583 ("You never saw"), 1617 ("one half"), 1621, 1622 ("very heavy").

16. James Breckenridge to John Breckinridge, June 13, 1788, diary of William Heth, June 25, 1788, in Kaminski et al., *Documentary History*, 10:1621 ("better adapted"), 1677 ("the scene").

17. Thomas Jefferson, "Account of the Bargain on the Assumption and Residence Bills," in Boyd et al., *Papers of Thomas Jefferson*, 17:205–7; Gordon S. Wood, *Empire of Liberty: A History of the Early Republic, 1789–1815* (New York: Oxford University Press, 2009), 92–109, 139–44.

18. Alan Taylor, "The Alien and Sedition Acts," in *The American Congress: The Building of Democracy*, ed. Julian E. Zelizer (Boston: Houghton Mifflin, 2004), 63–76; Wood, *Empire of Liberty*, 197–98.

19. James F. Simon, *What Kind of Nation: Thomas Jefferson, John Marshall, and the Epic Struggle to Create a United States* (New York: Simon and Schuster, 2002), 52–53, 57–62.

20. Thomas Jefferson to Elbridge Gerry, January 26, 1799, in Boyd et al., *Papers of Thomas Jefferson*, 30:645–53; Bruce Ackerman, *The Failure of the*

Founding Fathers: Jefferson, Marshall, and the Rise of Presidential Democracy (Cambridge MA: Harvard University Press, 2005), 97–99, 203–6; Peter S. Onuf, *Jefferson's Empire: The Language of American Nationhood* (Charlottesville: University of Virginia Press, 2000), 82, 100–102.

21. Ackerman, *Failure*, 100–108, 149–50; Onuf, *Jefferson's Empire*, 80–81, 85, 93, 107–8, 117–21; Simon, *What Kind of Nation*, 134–37, 150–51.

22. Haselby, *Origins*, 21–22; Pauline Maier, *American Scripture: Making the Declaration of Independence* (New York: W. W. Norton, 1990), 201–8; Simon, *What Kind of Nation*, 294–301.

23. For the celebration of the Founders as offering the antidote for modern politics, see Jill Lepore, *The Whites of Their Eyes: The Tea Party's Revolution and the Battle over American History* (Princeton NJ: Princeton University Press, 2010).

America's Broken Narrative of Exceptionalism

CODY DELISTRATY

I n 2009, while speaking to college students in Istanbul during his first official trip to Europe as president, Barack Obama admitted that America had in the past "made mistakes" and shown "flaws."[1] Just a few days before that, at a NATO press conference, he'd also said that "American exceptionalism" was no different from "British exceptionalism" or "Greek exceptionalism" and that America would no longer be making unilateral, bombastic decisions that would affect the globe under the guise of this myth.[2]

Unsurprisingly, his comments were met with pushback from American conservatives. Dick Cheney, speaking on Fox News' *Hannity*, characterized the president's comments as disrespecting the foundational philosophy of America and in doing so prostrating himself and his nation on the floor of the world.

"I think most of us believe, and most presidents believe, and talk about the truly exceptional nature of America," Cheney said. "There's never been a nation like the United States of America in world history, and yet you have a president who goes around and bows to his host and then proceeds to apologize profusely for the United States. I find that deeply disturbing."[3]

Besides Cheney trying to protect his own legacy as George W. Bush's warmongering vice president, implicit in his statement was that by dismissing American "exceptionalism" as similar to any other patriotic myth held by a multiplicity of countries, Obama was actively harming America. To disrepute American "exceptionalism" is not diplomacy but an act of "apology," the kissing of the grimy feet of another global power, in the view of Cheney and many others. For America to lose its sense of exceptionalism would be, in this view, to lose its very sense of history.

National narratives have existed, in one way or another, as far back as the nineteenth century. Benedict Anderson famously called a nation "an imagined community."[4] Eric Hobsbawm called it "an invented tradition."[5] Most relatively new nations have overarching myths about their foundation or national character. Australians, for instance, often point to the Gallipoli campaign during World War I: the character of their soldiers is a stand-in for their citizens' character.[6] The cult of character is an important one. Nineteenth-century American schoolchildren learned that George Washington couldn't tell a lie, that he came clean to his father about having chopped down a cherry tree. (It never happened; his biographer Parson Weems made it up for his semifictional biography, *The Life of Washington*. By any logical estimation, Washington was just as savvy and cutthroat as any other politician.)[7]

Corporations, too, have cults of character and foundational myths. Wal-Mart is a "family" company; Amazon started as a humble bookseller; Facebook began in a college dormitory.[8] But unlike nations, corporations have little incentive to depict themselves as exceptionally powerful. Just the opposite: they want to seem as friendly and nonmenacing as possible so you'll let them into your home as you would a friend.

Whereas newer nations like the United States tend to have overarching myths, older nations tend to have more "subnarratives"— specific politicized views on parts of their history that together portray their nation as consistently moral and strong, even as they've undergone numerous and significant changes. In France, for instance, a popular narrative that continues to persist is that the French resisted the Nazis en masse. Today, sculptures and placards and fountains attest to the bravery of the "resistance" throughout the country. The truth, of course, is that the Vichy government was a Nazi stronghold. Some parts of France capitulated to Nazi influence, and, as scholars like Robert Paxton and Robert Gildea have written about at length, there were many *collaborationnistes* as well—French people who actively sympathized with the Nazi cause and wanted to see it carried out.[9] (Even more recently, the French myth that the country had been "at war" with its colonies when in fact it had forcibly *colonized* them publicly lasted until former president François Hollande issued an apology to Algeria in 2012.)[10]

America, however, as both a powerful nation and a relatively new one, has not only cults of character and subnarratives but also overarching myths. There is the American Dream, the American West, the American Rise and Fall; and, like a savvy public relations company, America has defined itself to the rest of the world with phrases like the "shining city upon a hill" and the "leader of the free world."

America is also the only country whose myths so clearly inform its future. The American Dream is a myth that can refresh itself every generation so that, barring the cataclysmic, Americans will constantly believe they can "have it all" even as it's statistically—and increasingly—unlikely. "Perhaps a hundred years ago, America might have rightly claimed to have been the land of opportunity, or at least a land where there was more opportunity than elsewhere," wrote the economist Joseph Stiglitz. "But not for at least a quarter of a century. Horatio Alger–style rags-to-riches stories were not a deliberate hoax, but given how they've lulled us into a sense of complacency, they might as well have been."[11]

Similarly, there is a particular self-making mythos embraced by Americans. The American tale of growing up—the American Coming of Age story—is about the creation of a singular self, an individual who comes from nothing and can attain anything. Just as Hinduism in India is vital for retaining the caste system, this secular myth of self-creation is vital to a functioning capitalist, class-stratified system that cloaks itself in "meritocracy." As Stiglitz pointed out, "rags-to-riches stories" might as well have been "a deliberate hoax."[12] But foundational American ideas about hard work and, in more recent psychology parlance, "grit" are vital to maintaining socioeconomic class distinctions without inciting rebellion from those on society's lowest rungs. It's your own fault, these myths say to those who have been disadvantaged by social structures; you only need to work harder. This kind of social control hardly seems like the hallmark of an "exceptional" nation.

• • •

Ironically, it was Joseph Stalin who first coined the term "American exceptionalism" in 1929. When the leader of the American Communist Party, Jay Lovestone, told Stalin that the American working class wouldn't join in revolting, Stalin responded that they must end their "heresy of American exceptionalism."[13] Stalin, of course, meant it as a cut: American workers were betraying their own interests by believing they were different from the rest of the global proletariat. But the exceptionalism of America hadn't always seemed like a myth, and after World War II, when the United States defeated Nazi Germany, it became the most militarily and economically powerful country in the world. It also began to see itself as the most moral and virtuous. What Stalin had intended as ridicule came to be viewed as an accolade.

The myth was further popularized in 1980, when Ronald Reagan called America a "shining city upon a hill," launching the idea of America's global exceptionalism, the phrase a reference to an early seventeenth-century sermon given by John Winthrop, who, as the governor of the Massachusetts Bay Colony, had been imploring the Pilgrims to retain their Puritanism.[14] (Reagan added the "shining" part.) Between 1980 and 2000 the word "exceptionalism," as associated with America, showed up in national publications 457 times. From 2000 to 2010: 2,558 times. And in the three years between 2010 and 2012: an astounding 4,172 times.[15]

In the past few years, this myth has still been used to support a variety of suspect arguments. Obama's Affordable Care Act, for instance, was twisted by some conservatives to appear not as a moral and necessary type of health care reform but rather as a denigration of American exceptionalism, as an oppressor of "freedom." The Affordable Care Act is turning America "into a two-bit, second-rate, debt-laden European socialist backwater," wrote Monica Crowley, a Fox News contributor, in the conservative *Washington Times newspaper*. "We are exceptional Americans, and you are wholly unexceptional thieves of freedom. We want our liberty and exceptionalism back. We're throwing off the chains."[16]

In a way, it's impressive that this myth can be perverted in such a way that a country that finally decides to take care of its people's health can somehow seem like an enslavement. But it's hardly surprising. The myth of exceptionalism itself is oppressive and has long been so. In 1947 the French existentialist philosopher Jean-Paul Sartre noted that the myth seeps its way into American lives, changing our vision of happiness, even our vocabulary. "The system is a great external apparatus, an implacable machine which one might call the objective spirit of the United States and which over there they call Americanism—a huge complex of myths, values, recipes, slogans, figures, and rites," Sartre wrote. "There is this myth of happiness: black-magic slogans warn you to be happy at once; films that 'end well' show a life of rosy ease to the exhausted crowds; the language is charged with optimistic and unrestrained expressions—'have a good time,' 'life is fun,' and the like."[17]

But the myth has begun to shift in recent years. Exceptionalism, ever since Reagan first uttered it, has come to be married to capitalist liberalism. As it's defined by Republicans, exceptionalism tends to mean open markets no matter the cost; to Democrats, who embraced the myth during Hillary Clinton's failed 2016 presidential run, exceptionalism has tended to mean inclusiveness and identity politics while failing to address the fundamental economic issues facing many Americans.

Under President Donald Trump, however, the exceptionalism myth and its many submyths have begun to crumble. As Americans look around and see that their lives are broken, that they really can't ascend the socioeconomic ladder, that claims on morality can go either way, that America is no longer clearly an exceptional nation, they have turned toward the past—toward a former, fabricated "greatness."

"Americans are coming to realize that their cherished narrative of social and economic mobility is a myth," wrote Stiglitz. "Grand deceptions of this magnitude are hard to maintain for long—and the country has already been through a couple of decades of self-deception."[18]

What Trump has done so cleverly is to at once embrace and reject the myth. Americans are no longer exceptional, he seemed to say during his campaign; but we once were, and we could be again. A promised land has been lost, he seemed to say; with me it can be regained. This was the strategy of Alexander the Great. Of Jesus. Of Hitler. The long-standing myth that relies on a mis-remembering of the past always makes out the past to be golden and halcyon—but it also might be grasped again.

There was no golden American past, of course. Even during America's postwar prosperity, tens of millions of people suffered discrimination. It was golden only for a select few.

From the desire for a past that can never be attained comes either a deep cynicism—let's destroy everything, and hope-fully we can rebuild it better—or a desire to go even deeper into irrationality—we'll be safer and more prosperous if we milita-rize our borders. The myth is still used for all sorts of dubious reasons: to justify rigid class hierarchies, to justify wars and the abnegation of diplomacy, to oppose universal health care, to oppose telling the truth about history, or to conjure an ideal-ized past when few feel exceptional anymore. Yet, as poisonous as it can be, it is still possible to escape this myth, even as Trump continues to harp on clever variations of it.

"They struggle against it or they accept it," wrote Sartre about Americans and the exceptionalism myth. "They stifle in it or go beyond it; they submit to it or reinvent it; they give themselves up to it or make furious efforts to escape from it; in any case it remains outside them, transcendent, because they are men, and it is a thing."[19]

To believe we are exceptional is to fall into this trap. The myth, as Sartre says, remains outside of us. Even the best propaganda is only something that is continuously presented to us. We can always ignore it. But we must not only turn from it. With sober eyes, Americans must also look at our true history, the destruc-tion we've wreaked, the misery we've caused. Only once we've seen clearly how unexceptional we've often been might we finally move forward rather than trafficking in a phony past.

Notes

1. "Obama Asks World to Look Past U.S. Flaws," NBC News, April 7, 2009, www.nbcnews.com/id/30082531/ns/world_news-europe/t/obama-asks -world-look-past-us-stereotypes/#.WtIM0C-B3BJ.

2. James Fallows, "Obama on Exceptionalism," *Atlantic*, April 4, 2009.

3. Dick Cheney on *Hannity*, Fox News, December 9, 2009.

4. Benedict Anderson, *Imagined Communities: Reflections on the Origin and Spread of Nationalism* (London: Verso, 1983).

5. Eric Hobsbawm and Terence Ranger, *The Invention of Tradition* (New York: Cambridge University Press, 1983).

6. John Torode, "Gallipoli: Why Do Australians Celebrate a Military Disaster?," *BBC iWonder*, BBC, www.bbc.co.uk/guides/zyj4kqt.

7. Jay Richardson, "Cherry Tree Myth," George Washington's Mount Vernon, www.mountvernon.org/digital-encyclopedia/article/cherry-tree-myth.

8. "Our History," Walmart Corporate-We Save People Money So They Can Live Better, https://.corporate.walmart.com/our-story/our-history.

9. Robert O. Paxton, *La France de Vichy: 1940–1944* (Paris: Éditions du Seuil, 1974); Robert Gildea, *Marianne in Chains: Daily Life in the Heart of France during the German Occupation* (New York: Picador, 2004).

10. Associated Press in Algiers, "François Hollande Acknowledges Algerian Suffering under French Rule," *Guardian*, December 20, 2012.

11. Joseph E. Stiglitz, "Equal Opportunity, Our National Myth," *New York Times*, February 16, 2013, https://opinionator.blogs.nytimes.com/2013/02 /16/equal-opportunity-our-national-myth/.

12. Stiglitz, "Equal Opportunity."

13. Terrence McCoy, "How Joseph Stalin Invented 'American Exceptionalism,'" *Atlantic*, March 15, 2012, www.theatlantic.com/politics/archive/2012 /03/how-joseph-stalin-invented-american-exceptionalism/254534/.

14. "Ronald Reagan: Election Eve Address," American Presidency Project, www.presidency.ucsb.edu/ws/?pid=85199.

15. McCoy, "How Joseph Stalin."

16. Monica Crowley, "American Exceptionalism, RIP," *Washington Times*, March 23, 2010, www.washingtontimes.com/news/2010/mar/23/american -exceptionalism-rip.

17. Jean-Paul Sartre, "Americans and Their Myths," *Nation*, July 16, 2015, www.thenation.com/article/americans-and-their-myths.

18. Stiglitz, "Equal Opportunity."

19. Sartre, "Americans."

Contributors

Congressman **Jim Banks** serves on the House Armed Services; Veterans Affairs; and Science, Space, and Technology Committees. Prior to his election to Congress, Representative Banks was a member of the Indiana Senate. He joined the United States Navy Reserve as a supply corps officer and is an Afghanistan War veteran.

David W. Blight is professor of American history at Yale University and director of the Gilder Lehrman Center for the Study of Slavery, Resistance, and Abolition. Previously, Blight served as professor of history at Amherst College, where he taught for thirteen years. He has published many books and won many awards, including the Bancroft Prize and the Frederick Douglass Prize for *Race and Reunion*. His most recent book is *Frederick Douglass: Prophet of Freedom*.

Spencer Boyer is a senior fellow at the Penn Biden Center for Diplomacy & Global Engagement and a nonresident senior fellow in the Center on the United States and Europe at the Brookings Institution. From 2014 to 2017 he served in the Obama administration as national intelligence officer for Europe in the National Intelligence Council. Earlier, Boyer worked as deputy assistant secretary of state for European and Eurasian Affairs.

Eleanor Clift is a political reporter, television pundit, and author. She is a panelist on the public affairs show *The McLaughlin Group* and a columnist for *Daily Beast*. Clift formerly served as a *News-*

week White House, congressional, and political correspondent. She is the author or coauthor of several books and has appeared as herself in four feature films.

Joshua A. Claybourn is an attorney and the author or editor of several books, including *Abe's Youth: Collected Works from the Indiana Lincoln Inquiry* (coedited with William Bartelt). He has published widely on legal, political, and historical topics in a variety of popular press outlets, including *USA Today* and *The Hill*.

John C. Danforth is formerly U.S. senator from Missouri and U.S. ambassador to the United Nations. Before his election to the U.S. Senate, for eight years Danforth was attorney general for Missouri. Currently, he serves on the board of the nonprofit, nonpartisan Commission on Presidential Debates, as well as on the national advisory board of the John C. Danforth Center on Religion and Politics at Washington University. Danforth is an attorney, ordained Episcopal priest, and author of several books.

Cody Delistraty is a writer and historian based in Paris. He writes reported essays, cultural criticism, and profiles for the *New York Times*, the *New Yorker*, *New York*, *Frieze*, and the *Atlantic*, among others. He has degrees in history and politics from NYU and Oxford and was named one of the best young writers of the year by *British Vogue*.

Richard A. Epstein is the inaugural Laurence A. Tisch Professor of Law at New York University Law School, the Peter and Kirsten Bedford Senior Fellow at the Hoover Institution, and the James Parker Hall Distinguished Service Professor of Law Emeritus and Senior Lecturer at the University of Chicago. One of the most frequently cited American legal scholars, he is the author of numerous works, including *Takings* (1985), *Simple Rules for a Complex World* (1995), and *The Classical Liberal Constitution* (2014). Epstein is a member of the American Academy of Arts and Sciences and has received many awards, including the 2011 Bradley Prize, and was chosen in a poll by *Legal Affairs* as one of the most influential legal thinkers of modern times.

Nikolas Gvosdev is a professor of national security affairs at the U.S. Naval War College and the Captain Jerome E. Levy Chair in economic geography and national security. He is a senior fellow in the U.S. global engagement program at the Carnegie Council for Ethics and International Affairs. Gvosdev was previously editor of the *National Interest* and remains a senior editor at the magazine. He also holds a nonresidential senior fellowship at the Foreign Policy Research Institute. Gvosdev is the author or coauthor of several books on foreign policy and Russian-American international relations.

Cherie Harder serves as president of the Trinity Forum. Prior to joining the Trinity Forum in 2008, she served in the White House as special assistant to the president and director of policy and projects for First Lady Laura Bush. Earlier in her career Harder worked as policy advisor to Senate Majority Leader Bill Frist, advising him on domestic social issues and serving as liaison and outreach director to outside groups. From 2001 to 2005 she was senior counselor to the chairman of the National Endowment for the Humanities, where she helped design and launch the We the People initiative to enhance the teaching, study, and understanding of American history.

Jason Kuznicki is a research fellow with the Cato Institute, editor of Cato Books, and the editor of *Cato Unbound*, the Cato Institute's online journal of debate. He was an assistant editor of the *Encyclopedia of Libertarianism* and author of *Technology and the End of Authority: What Is Government For?*

Gerard N. Magliocca is the Samuel R. Rosen Professor at the Indiana University Robert H. McKinney School of Law. He is the author of four books. Magliocca regularly contributes to the legal blogs *Balkanization* and *Concurring Opinions* and is a member of the American Law Institute.

Markos Moulitsas is founder and publisher of *Daily Kos* and cofounder of Vox Media, a digital-media holding company with several editorial brands, including SB *Nation* and *Vox*. He is author or coauthor of several books, his latest being *45 Ways to Fight*

Trump. He previously served in the U.S. Army (1989–92) as a multiple launch rocket system operations / fire direction specialist.

Ilya Somin is a law professor at George Mason University and a blogger for the *Volokh Conspiracy* law and politics blog. His research focuses on constitutional law, property law, and the study of popular political participation and its implications for constitutional democracy. Somin has written many scholarly articles and books, including *Democracy and Political Ignorance: Why Smaller Government Is Smarter* and *The Grasping Hand: "Kelo v. City of New London" and the Limits of Eminent Domain*. Somin has also published articles in a variety of popular press outlets, including the *Wall Street Journal*, *Los Angeles Times*, *New York Times* Room for Debate website, CNN, USA *Today*, and US *News and World Report*.

Cass R. Sunstein is the Robert Walmsley University Professor at Harvard Law School, where he is founder and director of the Program on Behavioral Economics and Public Policy. He is by far the most frequently cited law professor in the United States. From 2009 to 2012 Sunstein served in the Obama administration as administrator of the White House Office of Information and Regulatory Affairs. He has testified before congressional committees, appeared on national television and radio shows, been involved in constitution-making and law-reform activities in several nations, and written many articles and books, including *Simpler: The Future of Government* and *Wiser: Getting Beyond Groupthink to Make Groups Smarter*. His best-selling book *Nudge*, written with Richard Thaler, helped lead to Thaler's 2017 Nobel Prize in Economic Sciences. Sunstein is a member of the American Academy of Arts and Sciences and the American Law Institute.

Alan Taylor is the Thomas Jefferson Memorial Foundation Professor of History at the University of Virginia. He is the author of many acclaimed books in early American history and twice received the Pulitzer Prize in History, once for *William Cooper's Town* and once for *The Internal Enemy*, the latter also a finalist for the National Book Award. Taylor taught earlier at Boston University and the University of California, Davis.

James V. Wertsch is the David R. Francis Distinguished Professor, vice chancellor for international affairs, and professor of anthropology at Washington University in St. Louis. He is also founding director of the McDonnell International Scholars Academy, Washington University's lead international initiative. Wertsch's research concerns language, thought, and culture, with a focus on national narratives and memory. He is the author of over two hundred publications appearing in over a dozen languages, including *Voices of the Mind*, *Mind as Action*, and *Voices of Collective Remembering*.

Gordon S. Wood is the Alva O. Way University Professor and Professor of History Emeritus at Brown University. His books include Pulitzer Prize–winning *The Radicalism of the American Revolution* and Bancroft Prize–winning *The Creation of the American Republic, 1776–1787*. He writes frequently for the *New York Review of Books* and the *New Republic*. In 2010 Wood received the National Humanities Medal. He is a fellow of the American Academy of Arts and Sciences and the American Philosophical Society.

Ali Wyne is a policy analyst at the nonprofit, nonpartisan RAND Corporation, a nonresident senior fellow with the Atlantic Council's Brent Scowcroft Center on International Security, and a security fellow with the Truman National Security Project.